THEMATIC UNIT
Spiders

D1613764

Written by Kathee Gosnell

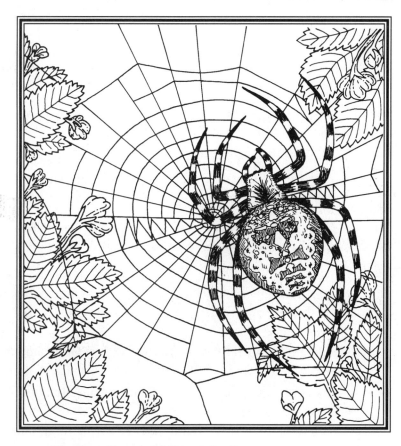

Teacher Created Materials, Inc.
6421 Industry Way
Westminster, CA 92683
www.teachercreated.com

©1995 Teacher Created Materials, Inc.
Reprinted, 2000

Made in U.S.A.

ISBN-1-55734-591-0

Illustrated by
Agi Palinay

Edited by
Walter Kelly, M.A.

Cover Art by
Agi Palinay

Table of Contents

Introduction

Spiders contains a captivating whole-language thematic unit about the study of arachnids as related to our understanding of the past and our hope for using this knowledge in the present to balance the eco-system in the future. These 80 exciting pages are filled with a wide variety of lesson ideas and reproducible pages designed for use with intermediate students. At its core this literature-based thematic unit has three high-quality children's literature selections: *Spiders, Eight Legs,* and *Charlotte's Web.* Also included are the summaries of seven folk tales which have spiders among the main characters. For each of these selections, activities are included which set the stage for reading, encourage the enjoyment of the selection, and extend the concepts gained. In addition, the theme is connected to the curriculum with activities in language arts, math, science, social studies, art, and life skills. Many of these activities encourage cooperative learning. Suggestions for bulletin board and unit management tools are additional time savers for the busy teacher. Highlighting this complete teacher resource is a culminating activity: Ballooning Journey. This activity allows students to synthesize and apply their knowledge beyond the classroom.

This thematic unit includes the following:

- ☐ **Literature selections** — summaries of three children's books and seven folk tales with related lessons (complete with reproducible pages) that cross the curriculum

- ☐ **Writing ideas** — daily suggestions, including Big Books, for writing across the curriculum

- ☐ **Group projects** — to foster cooperative learning

- ☐ **Bulletin board ideas** — suggestions and plans for student created and/or interactive bulletin boards

- ☐ **Planning guides** — suggestions for sequencing lessons each day of the unit

- ☐ **Curriculum connections** — in language arts, math, science, social studies, art, and life skills

- ☐ **Culminating activities** — to help students synthesize their learning

- ☐ **Bibliography** — suggestions for additional books on the theme

---

To keep this valuable resource intact so it can be used year after year, you may wish to punch holes in the pages and store them in a three-ring binder.

Introduction *(cont.)*

Why Whole Language?

A whole-language approach involves children using all modes of communication: reading, writing, listening, observing, illustrating, and speaking. Communication skills are integrated into lessons which emphasize the whole of language rather than isolating its parts. A child reads, writes (spelling appropriately for his/her level), speaks, listens, and thinks in response to a literature experience introduced by the teacher. In this way, language skills grow naturally, stimulated by involvement and interest in the topic at hand.

Why Thematic Planning?

One useful tool for implementing an integrated whole-language program is thematic planning. By choosing a theme with corresponding literature selections for a unit of study, a teacher can plan activities throughout the day that lead to a cohesive, in-depth study of the topic. Students practice and apply their skills in meaningful contexts. Consequently, they tend to learn and retain more. Both teachers and students are freed from a day that is broken into unrelated segments of isolated drill and practice.

Why Cooperative Learning?

In addition to academic skills and content, students need to learn social skills. No longer can this area of development be taken for granted. Students must learn to work cooperatively in groups in order to function well in modern society. Group activities should be a regular part of school life, and teachers should consciously include social objectives as well as academic objectives in their planning. The teacher should clarify and monitor the qualities of good group interaction just as he/she would clarify and monitor the academic goals of a project.

Why Big Books?

An excellent cooperative whole-language activity is the production of Big Books. Groups of students or the entire class can apply their language skills and content knowledge to create additions to the classroom library. These books make excellent culminating projects for sharing beyond the classroom with parents and friends. This thematic unit includes directions for making Big Books in your classroom.

Spiders

by Jane Dallinger

Summary

Spiders are not insects. They belong to a group of animals called arachnids. Our selection by Jane Dallinger is a Lerner Natural Science book. It received a Children's Science Book Award. You will learn how spiders differ from insects. For example, spiders have eight legs, while insects have only six. You will learn about other differences also.

How do spiders spin webs? Why do they spin webs? Do all spiders spin webs? How do spiders reproduce? What do spiders eat? Who are spiders' enemies? These are some questions you may ask and for which you will find the answers in this book, *Spiders*.

The outline below is a suggested plan for using the various activities that are presented in this unit. You should adapt these ideas to fit your own classroom situation.

Sample Plan

Day 1

- Read pages 3–22.
- Have 15 minutes of silent sustained reading (SSR) (page 6).
- Complete the crossword puzzle (page 49).
- Do the completion puzzle (page 8).

Day 2

- Read pages 24–34.
- Have SSR.
- Write a Natural Science Journal magazine article (page 9).
- Solve the triangle web addition (page 53).

Day 3

- Read pages 36–47.
- Have SSR.

- Introduce daily writing topics (page 40).
- Discover spider facts (page 10).
- Complete the bar graph (page 58).

Day 4

- Have SSR.
- Continue daily writing topics (page 40).
- Identify the body of a spider (page 11).
- Map tarantulas in the U.S. (page 66).

Day 5

- Have SSR.
- Continue daily writing topics (page 40).
- Research and fill in the Venn diagram (page 12).
- Complete the scientific crossword puzzle (page 62).
- Share spider safety facts (page 72).

Overview of Activities

Setting the Stage

1. Prepare your classroom for a unit on arachnids. Collect books, magazines, and pamphlets on arachnids, spiders, spider webs, and folk tales about the same. (See word bank listings on page 48 and the bibliography, page 77, for ideas).

2. Brainstorm with the students to see how much they know about spiders and other arachnids. Put an idea web on the chalkboard and let the students express their ideas about spiders and arachnids while you write them down. After they have finished brainstorming, have them copy the web into their writer's workbook (page 39). After the end of this thematic unit, have them do this exercise again so they may compare and contrast what they have learned.

3. Introduce Writer's Workbook (page 39). Emphasize "clue words" which will help trigger a string of ideas. Discuss the importance of taking just enough notes to understand the information a week later. Read information from a pamphlet or encyclopedia to the class and have them practice taking notes. Have the students write only one word or phrase in their writers' workbooks.

4. Begin Silent Sustained Reading (SSR). Plan a 15-20 minute period each day for SSR. Have each student read a book or article about spiders, arachnids, arachnologists, or other related natural science material. For examples, see word bank listings (page 48) and the bibliography (page 77). Give 15 minutes of reading homework, and set a date for books to be finished. In their writers' workbooks or on loose-leaf paper, have students take notes on the books they are reading. Then have them place the notes in their folders.

5. Introduce writing topics for *Spiders* (page 40).

Enjoying the Book

1. Read and discuss pages 3–22 in *Spiders*. Talk about spiders and where they can be found. Tell the students that there are 30,000 to 40,000 different kinds of spiders found all over the world. All of them are able to produce silk. Discuss some of the different types of webs that spiders weave. Complete the crossword puzzle (page 49). Students will learn some interesting facts when they fill in the completion puzzle (page 8).

2. Read and discuss pages 24–34. Talk about how spiders eat and why they poison their prey. Discuss ways spiders capture prey other than with webs. Mention the balance of nature and the spider's part in it. Don't forget the enemies of spiders, too. Write the Natural Science Journal magazine article (page 9). Solve the triangle web addition puzzle (page 53).

Overview Of Activities *(cont.)*

Enjoying the Book *(cont.)*

3. Read and discuss pages 36–47. Go over the glossary terms in the back of the book. Introduce daily writing topics (page 40). Discover more spider facts by completing the puzzle on page 10. Compare spider lengths by means of a bar graph on page 58.

4. Continue daily writing topics (page 40). Identify the parts of a spider body (page 11). Find out where tarantulas are located in the U.S. Color the map accordingly (page 66).

5. Continue daily writing topics (page 40). Research to find the differences between insects and spiders. Compare and contrast by means of the Venn diagram (page 12). Complete the scientific crossword puzzle (page 62).

Extending the Book

1. Invite local zoologists, arachnologists, or entomologists into your classroom. Have them discuss their area of expertise. Talk about the balance of nature. Encourage them to bring slides or video tapes or collections to show the class.

2. Have students make books (pages 43–47) on ideas from the word bank (page 48) or from the selection or other related subjects that follow this thematic unit.

3. Research and find out more about spider webs. Plan a field trip, if possible, to search for webs.

4. Study spider safety as a necessary part of living on a planet with other creatures (page 72). Humans have few—if any—natural enemies in this world. Nevertheless, we can suffer from attacks by other creatures if we purposely or in ignorance invade their territory or appear to threaten their safety.

   • Learn to identify the appearance, size, and habitat of dangerous spiders like the black widow and brown recluse.

   • Study the danger signs and first-aid procedures for suspected poisonous spider bites.

   • Make posters about spider safety to take home for reference and family use.

5. Build individual and class collections of spider pictures and names.

   • Include their scientific classifications into kingdom, phylum, class, family, genus, and species.

   • Use index cards to build a class reference file available to all students and parents. (This makes an excellent display of student-produced activity during any parent visitation or open house.)

   • Add sketches or pictures of typical web structures for each species.

Completion Puzzle

Fill in the blanks below using the word bank at the bottom of the page. The circled letter in each answer spells a word that will complete the sentence (number 10) at the bottom of the puzzle.

1. The __ __ __ __ ◯ __ __ __ __ __ __ __ __ __ is one of the two main parts of the spider's body.

2. __ __ __ __ __ __ __ ◯ __ __ __ are small tubes through which silk threads leave the spider's body.

3. They are located at the back of the second main part of the spider's body, the ◯ __ __ __ __ __ __.

4. Spiders wrap their eggs in silk egg sacs called __ __ ◯ __ __ __ __.

5. Silk __ ◯ __ __ __ __ __ are also used to make webs.

6. __ __ ◯ __ __ is a poison used to paralyze insects.

7. As spiderlings grow, they shed their outer skin several times. This is called __ __ __ __ ◯ __ __.

8. A young spider is called a __ __ __ ◯ __ __ __ __ __ __ __.

9. __ __ ◯ __ __ __ __ are the main food of spiders.

10. __ __ __ __ __ __ __ __ __ are the group of animals to which spiders belong.

Word Bank

abdomen * cephalothorax * cocoons * insects * molting

spiderling * spinnerets * threads * venom

8

Natural Science Journal Magazine Article

Pretend you are a writer for a natural science journal. It is your assignment to write a brief account of an interview with an arachnologist and the discovery of a new spider whose venom is being used to cure certain forms of cancer. It is to be part of a feature presentation entitled: "What's Happening in the World of Arachnology."

Use the five W's—who, where, when, what, why—to relate the information needed in your summary. Use your imagination to create this article. Be fanciful, but remember—it is a science journal. Also remember it is to be a brief account. Create an interesting title to catch the eye of your reader.

- **Who:** Include the name and background of your interviewee.

- **Where:** Tell exactly where these events took place in the world.

- **When:** Include the times (dates) when the events began and ended.

- **What happened:** Choose the most important events to focus on.

- **Why it is noteworthy:** There may be more than one reason. Be specific about your explanation.

- **Extra details:** Sometimes colorful details will add humor and/or dramatic interest.

Write your article in the space below, continuing on the back of the page if you need more space.

Title

Spider Facts

To find out some interesting facts about spiders, solve the problems below. Then write the letter that is beside each answer every time you find that answer in the puzzle below.

45x11 = _____ =A	618+15 = _____ =B	143–13 = _____ =C	59–12 = _____ =H
16x12 = _____ =E	28+73 = _____ =F	198÷22 = _____ =G	999–431 = _____ =L
61x4 = _____ =I	38+18 = _____ =J	128–16 = _____ =K	875–758 = _____ =P
15x3 = _____ =M	77+13 = _____ =N	357÷7 = _____ =O	567–222 = _____ =T
29x8 = _____ =Q	705+23 = _____ =R	354÷6 = _____ =S	111–99 = _____ =X
26x13 = _____ =U	532+27 = _____ =V	185÷5 = _____ =W	
41x11 = _____ =Y	519+111= _____ =Z	315–111= _____ =D	

1. Spiders that make orb webs are called orb ___ ___ ___ ___ ___ ___ ___ .
37   192   495   559   192   728   59

2. Spider webs are traps for catching insects, which are the   ___ ___ ___ ___ of spiders.
117   728   192   451

3. A purse web looks like a long   ___ ___ ___ ___ .
345   338   633   192

4. A ___ ___ ___ ___ ___ ___ thread goes from a hiding spider to the
59   244   9   90   495   568
spider's web. Any vibration alerts the spider that something is on the web.

5. Spider venom does not usually hurt   ___ ___ ___ ___ ___ ___ . There are a few spiders,
47   338   45   495   90   59
such as black widows, which are poisonous to humans.

6. A trap-door spider lives in a ___ ___ ___ ___ ___ ___ with silk-and-dirt doors.
633   338   728   728   51   37

7. Spiders protect the balance of   ___ ___ ___ ___ ___ ___ by eating insects.
90   495   345   338   728   192

8. Most spiders have eight   ___ ___ ___ ___ on their heads, but some have only six,
192   451   192   59
four, two, or none.

9. Spiderlings have the ability to   ___ ___ ___ ___ a new leg if an old one is lost.
9   728   51   37

10. ___ ___ ___ ___ ___ ___ ___ ___ ___ ___ ___ is a method of travel used by spiders.
633 495   568   568   51   51 50   90 244   90   9
The wind, blowing their silk threads, floats them through the air like a balloon.

Identify the Body of a Spider

Identify the body of a spider using the words below.

Word Bank

abdomen ✳ cephalothorax ✳ claw ✳ eyes ✳ fang ✳ leg ✳ spinnerets

The Body of a Spider

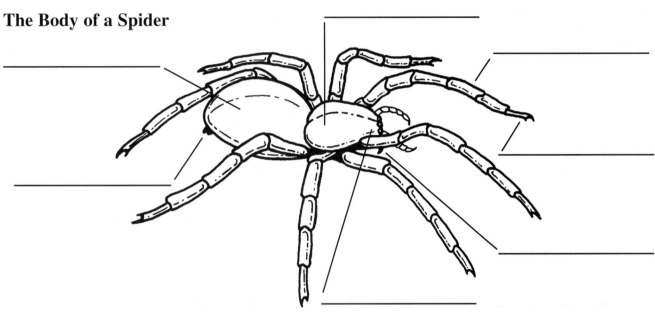

Answer the questions below.

1. What are the two main parts of the spider's body?

    _____

2. Which part has the wings and antennae?

    _____

3. Why do spiders have glands that make poison?

    _____

4. Is the silk that spiders produce all the same type?

    _____

5. How many legs does a spider have?

    _____

6. How many eyes does a spider have?

    _____

Venn Diagram

Use your knowledge about spiders and insects to fill in the circles below with information about each. In the space in the center where the circles join, write things that spiders and insects have in common. In the other parts of the circles, write things they do not have in common.

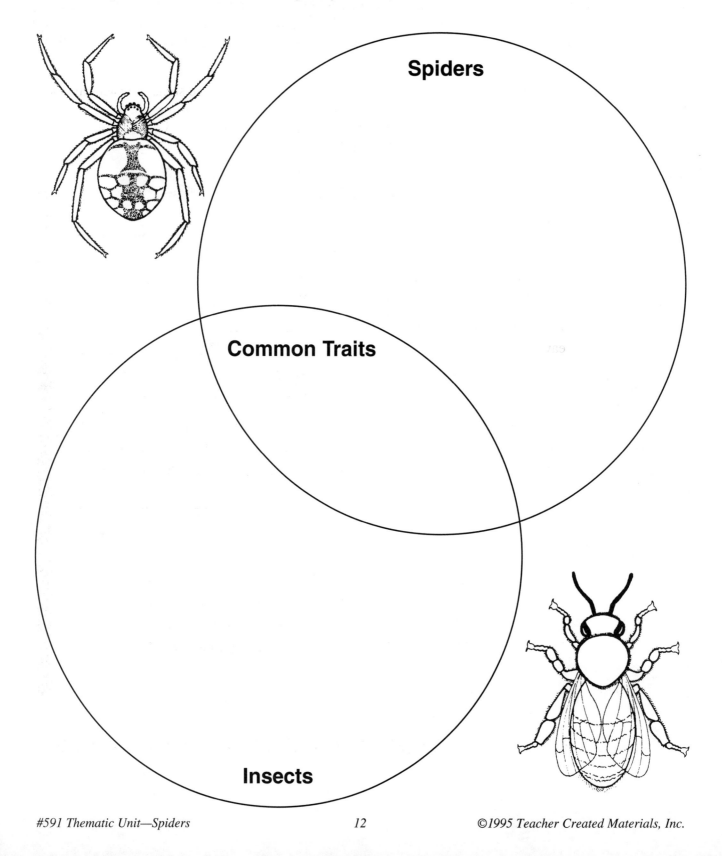

Spiders

Common Traits

Insects

Eight Legs
by D.M. Souza

Summary

If you know anything about spiders, you should know that they have eight legs. In this selection, you will learn about a few of the 40,000 known types of spiders and other eight-legged creatures that belong to the class of arachnids. Harvestmen (daddy-longlegs), scorpions, mites, and ticks also belong to this class.

For the most part, these arachnids are harmless, helpful creatures. But there are some to watch out for. You don't need to have arachnophobia (being deathly afraid of arachnids), but you can be informed as to which eight-legged creatures can cause painful bites. You can find some of this information in this selection, *Eight Legs* from the "Creatures All Around Us" series.

Sample Plan

Day 1

- Read pages 3–16.
- Have SSR.
- Introduce daily writing topics (page 40).
- Do the web weavers puzzle (page 18).
- Develop homonym "cents" about tarantulas (page 52).

Day 2

- Read pages 17–24.
- Have SSR.
- Continue daily writing topics (page 40).
- Unscramble the words to discover spider facts (page 15).
- Do the spider/web math matchup (page 54).

Day 3

- Read pages 26–31.
- Have SSR.
- Continue daily writing topics (page 40).

- Find out more about black widow spiders (page 16).
- Map black widows throughout the world (page 64).

Day 4

- Read pages 32–39.
- Have SSR.
- Continue daily writing topics (page 40).
- Complete the arachnids puzzle (page 17).
- Do the arachnid word search (page 50).

Day 5

- Have SSR.
- Continue daily writing topics (page 40).
- Discover spider superstitions (page 67).
- Study spider safety (page 72).
- Investigate household hazards (page 73).

Overview of Activities

Setting the Stage

1. Introduce daily writing topics for *Eight Legs* (page 40).

2. Put up a bulletin board appropriate for this section to display exceptional papers. See Bulletin Board Ideas (page 75) or use one of your own good ideas.

3. Introduce the words from the arachnids word bank (page 48).

Enjoying the Book

1. Read and discuss pages 3–16 in our selection, *Eight Legs*. Continue daily writing topics (page 40). Do the web weavers puzzle (page 18). Find the misused homonyms in the activity Homonym "Cents" About Tarantulas (page 52). You may decide to extend the exercise by having a contest to see who can list the most homonyms. You may decide to set a time limit.

2. Read and discuss pages 17–24. Continue daily writing topics (page 40). Discuss the hunters and fishers that appear in this section. Talk about the camouflage of these and other spiders. Unscramble the words to discover spider facts (page 15). Do the spider/web math matchup (page 54).

3. Read and discuss pages 26–31. Continue daily writing topics (page 40). Find out more about black widow spiders by completing the exercise on page 16. Where are black widows found throughout the world? Research and then complete the world map (page 64).

4. Read and discuss pages 32–39. Review the glossary terms on page 39. Continue daily writing topics (page 40). Learn more facts about arachnids by solving the completion activities on page 17. Do the arachnid word search (page 50).

5. Continue daily writing topics (page 40). Find out about spider superstitions (page 67).

Extending the Book

1. Plan a field trip to search for arachnids. Try several different areas where the habitat differs. Explain how the arachnids differ from area to area. Describe their surroundings. Try also to discover their food sources. Watch for nests and egg sacs.

2. Have students make books (page 43) on ideas from the word bank (page 48) or from our selection.

3. Research possible hazards of the most common methods of spider and insect control (page 73).

    *   Brainstorm lists of pest control methods.

    *   Brainstrom lists of common pesticides.

    *   Prepare a home inventory of poisons, contents, locations, warnings, and antidotes.

    *   Prepare a sample home inventory as a chart or bulletin board display.

14

Unscramble

Unscramble the words below each line to make a new word that will provide you with more information about spiders.

1. Spiders belong to a class of animals called _____.
    chaindsra

2. Spiders' bodies are divided into two parts—the cephalothorax and the _____.
    dabenom

3. Spiders use the _____ , or setae (SEE-tee), on their legs to help them sense
    shrai
    what is surrounding them.

4. A spider cannot chew or swallow solids. They use their _____ , or chelicerae
    swaj

    (kuh-LIS-uh-ree), to hold their victims while sharp fangs inject a poisonous liquid.

5. This poisonous liquid is called _____.
    novem

6. Under the spider's abdomen are two openings called spiracles (SPIH-ruh-kuhlz) that help it
    _____.
    threabe

7. As a spider grows to adulthood, it sheds its soft, stretchy outer covering, or cuticles (KYOO-tih-
    kuhlz). This is called _____.
    tomnigl

8. A _____ is a silk line that spiders attach to objects as they move from place to
    graldine
    place. It helps them to get back to webs or nests.

9. _____ is a method the spiderlings use to travel away from the place they hatch.
    lolobannig

10. Not all spiders spin webs to catch prey. Others are _____ and fishers.
    stunrhe

11. Crab spiders are hunters that can move backwards and sideways like a crab. Many hide in
    flowers and are the same _____ as the flowers, blending into the background.
    crool

12. Female spiders are usually _____ than males.
    gregbi

Black Widow Spiders

1. Most spiders are poisonous, but only two spiders in the United States are dangerous to humans. They are the brown recluse spider and the black widow spider.

2. There are five different species of widow spiders that live in the U.S. There is a brown widow, a red widow, and three kinds of black widow spiders.

3. All black widow spiders belong to a family called Theridiidae, the comb-footed spiders. They weave irregular, tangled webs. Only the females are poisonous to humans.

4. Adult female black widows are a shiny black color with red markings on their bellies. If a black widow is hungry, she may eat her mate.

5. The widow spider may make as many as nine egg sacs, each containing about 250 eggs. She will protect her egg sacs by holding on to them with her front legs. She will also protect them from the weather.

6. When the spiderlings hatch, they had better leave in a hurry. Mama may eat many of them before they go ballooning.

7. Males mature faster than females, but they live only about four months. Females often live a year or longer.

8. The silk from black widows has been used in telescopes, gunsights, and laboratory and surveying equipment.

9. Few people die from black widow bites. Children and older people are more affected. Your chances of dying from a bite are about the same as your chances of being struck by lightning.

Read the article above. Then write the number of the line(s) which contains the answer to questions below. Finally, write the answers in the spaces after the questions. Use the back of the paper if you need more room.

1. _____ Are there any dangerous spiders in the U.S.? _____

2. _____ Which is more dangerous—the male or female black widow? _____

3. _____ Do spiders eat other spiders? _____

4. _____ What uses have been made from spider silk? _____

5. _____ How long do spiders live? _____

6. _____ Do many people die from spider bites? _____

7. _____ What family does the black widow belong to? _____

8. _____ How many species of widow spiders live in the U.S.? _____

Arachnids

Some arachnids are described below. Write the name of each in the space provided—a letter has been added to help you. Use the word bank at the bottom of the page.

1. The __ __ r __ __ __ spider is an orb weaver. It spins beautiful wheel-shaped webs.

2. The American __ o __ __ __ spider is a comb-footed spider.

3. One of the jumping spiders is a __ __ b __ __ spider. Before jumping, the spider secures a silk thread on which it can climb back in case it misses its mark.

4. __ r __ __ spiders are hunters. Many are the same color as the flowers they hide in.

5. A female __ o __ __ spider will carry her hatched spiderlings on her back for almost a week until they molt.

6. Female nursery-web spiders, a type of __ __ s __ __ __ __ spider, carry their egg sacs around with them in their jaws.

7. __ a __ __ __ __ __ __ __ __ are not spiders, but they are arachnids. They are commonly known as daddy longlegs.

8. __ c __ __ __ __ __ __ __ look more like lobsters than spiders.

9. __ h __ __ __ __ __ __ __ __ __ __ have no stingers but have large grasping palps.

10. Many __ __ t __ __ are parasites on plants or animals.

11. __ i __ __ __ are the largest of the mites. They are external parasites of reptiles, birds, or mammals. Some types transmit diseases such as Lyme's Disease.

Word Bank

crab ✳ fishing ✳ garden ✳ harvestmen ✳ house ✳ mites ✳ scorpions
ticks ✳ whipscorpions ✳ wolf ✳ zebra

Web Weavers

In the puzzle below, you will find 15 different types of spiders. Using the names listed in the word bank, locate and outline each name. You will find the names appear in diagonal and zig-zag lines, but never backwards or upside down. Some will share a letter as in a crossword puzzle.

example:

```
c     r     a     b
o
m
b
```

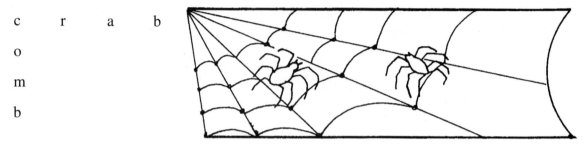

After outlining, use a crayon or marker to fill in your outlines. You will have a web when you are finished, and the letters that are left will spell a word naming what the spiders would hope to catch in a web.

Word Bank

black widow ✳ garden ✳ crab ✳ jumping ✳ wolf ✳ zebra ✳ huntsman ✳ orb weaver
nursery web ✳ fishing ✳ grass ✳ trap-door ✳ purse web ✳ comb footed ✳ tarantula

---

```
                              t
                        a   r   a   n
               g     s   e   r   y   w   e       t
      c    n   u   r               b       u       f
        r           a   c   k   w   i   d   j           l
        a       l       s               o   u   o       a
   g  a  r   b           s       o           w   m           n   g
        d           b               r               p   i
        e                   u           b   w   e   a   v   e   r
      h   u   n   t   s   r       g       f   i   s   h
          c   o   m   a   n   s   z   d       i
              o                       e           n
              d   m   b   f   o   o   t       b           g
        p   u   r                           r
      a           s   e   w   e   b               a
   r
t
```

Folk Tale Summaries

Spiders play an important role in the lives of people all over the world. This fact becomes especially apparent in the mythical, magical legends that have been handed down from generation to generation in folk tales from Japan, America, Africa, and points in between. The very word *weave* connects storytelling with spiders. It can mean to form a story or poem, or to make or spin a web. The following are summaries of spider tales woven into the folklore traditions of several countries. Check the bibliography (page 77) to find books of these folk tales and others.

The White Spider's Gift

This tale is told by the Guarani Indians of Paraguay. It tells of an Indian boy who rescues a tiny white spider from drowning. Many years later, the spider returns the kindness by helping the now-grown Indian boy win the hand of a beautiful Indian princess in marriage. The Spider spins a glorious web complete with designs of birds, orchids, begonias, and other flowers. When it is complete, the web becomes a mantle of shimmering lace. With this gift—this treasure beyond compare—the Indian brave wins the princess as his bride. She wears the lace mantle as a veil and inspires the women of the village to try to weave the same beautiful lace on their looms.

The women of the villages in Paraguay are still making *ñandutí,* or spider's web lace—famous throughout the world for its delicate beauty.

How Spider Taught Women to Weave

This is a tale from Argentina. Ponchos are important, practical types of clothing worn by many in Latin America. A poncho looks like a blanket with a hole cut in the middle. It is slipped on over the head. It is worn to keep people warm and dry.

Two old women steal Spider's bag of thread and try to duplicate it. They try yuchan pods, but that does not work. They can not make thread from it. They try many other things but have no luck. They finally decide that they need sheep's wool. After many troubles, they succeed in getting the wool, spinning the thread, and weaving it into cloth for ponchos for everyone.

19

Folk Tale Summaries *(cont.)*

Anansi, the Spider Man

The tales of Anansi, who was a man and a spider, were stories told in the villages and forests of West Africa. When slave traders began kidnapping the villagers and taking them to the islands of the Caribbean, the Africans brought with them the stories they loved. These stories of Anansi are not only African folk tales but also Jamaican folk tales.

Anansi was considered to be a trickster. He always got the better of those who were much bigger than he. Long, long ago, all stories belonged to the Sky God. Anansi went to buy the stories. The Sky God wanted a python, a fairy, and 47 hornets for them. It sounded like a difficult amount to pay, but Anansi thought of a plan. He managed to tie up the foolish python. Then he came up with a plan to capture the fairy with sticky sap and a doll. How do you manage to get 47 hornets? Anansi found a gourd that was the same size and shape as a hornet's nest. He made a plug for the neck. He fooled the hornets into thinking the rains had come. They began to fly into the gourd. When 47 had flown in, Anansi put in the plug and took the gourd and hornets to the Sky God. The Sky God was impressed! He announced that the Sky God stories now belonged to Anansi and would be called Spider Stories.

Arachne

Arachne is a skilled weaver in Greek mythology. Athena is the goddess of arts and crafts. Arachne bragged that she could weave fabrics more beautiful than those woven by Athena. Athena heard of these boasts. She disguised herself as an old woman and warned Arachne not to brag so much. Arachne ignored her advice with scorn. Then Athena revealed herself as a goddess and accepted Arachne's challenge to a weaving contest.

Athena wove a tapestry that pictured mortals being punished by the gods for their pride. Arachne's tapestry showed the shocking misbehavior of gods and goddesses. When Athena saw that Arachne's work was as beautiful as her own, she tore it up in anger and jealousy. Arachne was terrified and tried to hang herself. Athena felt sorry for her and transformed her into a spider. Arachne's skill continues when her offspring, the spiders, spin their webs.

20

Waka-onna Noh Mask
Noh is a dramatic art form unique to Japan, with a history of about 600 years. This Noh mask of a young woman was crafted by Deme Yuusuiyasuhisa during the middle of the Edo Period (1615-1867). 6.8 cm deep X 13.8 cm wide X 21.3 cm high. Property of the Umewaka Kennōkai Foundation.

Folk Tale Summaries *(cont.)*

The Spider Weaver

This is a Japanese tale. It is about a young farmer who saves a spider from a snake which is about to eat it. One morning not long after that, a young girl comes to his home. She wants to work for him weaving cloth. The young farmer is pleased and gives her a job. At the end of the day, he is surprised to find that she has woven eight long pieces of cloth, enough for eight kimonos. He has never known anyone who could weave so much in just one day.

When the farmer asks her how she could weave so much, she tells him that he must never ask her that. And he is not supposed to come into the weaving room while she is at work. The farmer's curiosity gets the better of him, so he peeks into the window. There at the loom is a large spider, weaving very fast with its eight legs. The farmer notices that the spider is the very one he had rescued from the snake. This is how the spider is repaying his kindness.

When he notices that the cotton is almost used up, he goes to get some more. As he stops to rest on the way back home, a snake—the same one he chased away from the spider—crawls inside the cotton.

When the farmer gets back home, he gives the cotton to the weaving girl/spider. After the farmer leaves the room, she changes back into the spider and begins to eat the cotton so she can spin it into thread inside her body.

When the spider nears the end of the bundle, the snake jumps out at her. When it opens its mouth wide to swallow her, she jumps out the window. The snake chases her and catches up with her because she is so full of cotton. Just as the snake is about to get her, Old Man Sun rescues her. He reaches out with a sunbeam, catches the end of the web, and pulls her into the sky.

The spider is so grateful for having been saved that she uses up all the cotton in her body to weave beautiful fleecy clouds up in the sky. To this day in Japan, soft white cottony clouds and spiders are called by the same name: kumo!

Folk Tale Summaries *(cont.)*

Spider Woman

Among some of the Indian tribes in the Southwestern United States—Arizona, New Mexico, Colorado, and Utah—Spider Woman plays an important role in the mythology of their societies.

In the Navajo stories of creation, Spider Woman helps the twin sons of Changing Woman. It is Changing Woman who made the first Navajo people. The Glittering World in which they lived was unsafe because it was filled with monsters. The twin boys (Child Born of Water and Monster Slayer) set out to kill the monsters.

One day while they are hunting, the twins hear a voice coming from a small hole in the ground. The voice bids them come inside. The hole grows larger so the twins can enter. In the hole, they meet Spider Woman. She helps the twins to find their father, the Sun, who will assist them in slaying the monsters. First the boys have a dangerous journey to contend with, and then they have dangerous tests to prove themselves to their father. Because Spider Woman has prepared them, the boys pass their tests.

The Sun rewards them with weapons. To Monster Slayer, the Sun gives Lightning That Strikes Crooked. To Child Born of Water, he gives Lightning That Flashes Straight. With these weapons, the boys are able to kill all the monsters, except for those that cause old age, hunger, lice, and death. (Those four make you wonder what the other monsters are.) So with thanks to Spider Woman and Changing Woman's sons, the Glittering World became safe for the Navajo people.

How Grandmother Spider Stole the Sun

The Navajo and Hopi had Spider Woman. The Zuni and the Muskogee told stories of Grandmother Spider. This is a story the Muskogee tell of how the sun was brought around to the dark side of the Earth.

The animals decided to steal a piece of the Sun. Fox was the first to try, but he burned his mouth. Now all foxes have black mouths. Possum was next. She hid it in her bushy tail. The Sun was so hot it burned off all the hair on her tail. To this day, all possums have bare tails.

Then Grandmother Spider tried. She wove a bag out of her webbing. She put a piece of the Sun into the bag and carried it back with her. No one knew what to do with it then. Grandmother Spider said the Sun should be up high in the sky. Then everyone would be able to see it, and the light would benefit everyone.

Buzzard could fly the highest, so he put the Sun on top of his head and he began to fly toward the top of the sky. The Sun burned through Grandmother Spider's bag, burned away all of Buzzard's feathers on top of his head, and turned his head red. Buzzard was honored by all the birds and animals. He is still the highest flyer of all and still can be seen circling the Sun.

Grandmother Spider is honored at times when the Sun makes rays across the sky shaped like the rays in her web. It reminds us all of what Grandmother Spider did for everyone, and that we are all connected like the strands of her web.

Folk Tale Summaries *(cont.)*

Background

Folk tales have a compelling attraction for all people. Scholars tell us that their origins are anchored deep in the past, a past from which the rich and varied cultures of our planet have produced a colorful tapestry of fable, story, and legend.

Unique among the fables of our common humanity are the spider tales. These tales reflect our admiration for the boundless industry of that tiny creature, the beauty of its silken artistry, the practicality of its weaving, the marvelous engineering of its web, the shrewdness of its plans, the amazing ability to produce an endless thread from within its body, the craftiness of trapping its victim. In short, we seem to have found in the spider a rich source of symbolism and metaphor to apply to our own lives.

Yes, we owe much to those who created these tales, the ones who knew that all humanity loves a good story, especially one with strands reaching into our own lives. Such tales capture us like the spider's web, connecting us in a common human family of humor, wonder, warmth, and awe.

Sample Plan

Day 1

- Read the introduction to Folk Tale Summaries, *The White Spider's Gift* and *How Spider Taught Women to Weave* (page 19).
- Have SSR.
- Introduce daily writing topics (page 41).
- Design your own spider's web lace (page 26).
- Discover your fear factor—arachnophobia (page 51).

Day 2

- Read the Anansi summary (page 20).
- Have SSR.
- Continue daily writing topics (page 41).
- Sequence *Anansi, The Spider Man* (page 27).
- Discover the living fossils: scorpions (page 68).

Day 3

- Read the *Spider Weaver* summary (page 21).
- Have SSR.
- Continue daily writing topics (page 41).

- Answer true or false questions about the *Spider Weaver* (page 28).
- Do math mystery match (page 55).

Day 4

- Read the Arachne summary (page 20).
- Have SSR.
- Continue daily writing topics (page 41).
- Develop constellation creations (page 25).
- Do It's In the Stars (pages 70-71).

Day 5

- Read the *Spider Woman* and *How Grandmother Spider Stole the Sun* summaries (page 22).
- Have SSR.
- Continue daily writing topics (page 41).
- Organize team writing (page 29).
- Practice storytelling (page 30).
- Discuss scientific classification (pages 59–61).

Overview of Activities

Setting the Stage
---

1. Introduce daily writing topics for folk tales. (page 41)

2. Put up a bulletin board appropriate for this section to display exceptional papers. See Bulletin Board Ideas (page 75) or use one of your own good ideas.

3. Read the short introduction to the folk tales summaries (page 19). Discuss what a folk tale is. Have students name folk tales they may know. Ask them why folk tales are an important part of our history. Explain to them that stories were around much longer than the written word. Mention that the tales change at every telling. Parts are added or deleted as the storyteller desires. You will find many folk tale books listed in the bibliography (page 77) if you are interested in reading more about the stories that the summaries are based on.

Enjoying the Book
---

1. Read and discuss the summaries of *The White Spider's Gift* and *How Spider Taught Women To Weave* (page 19). Continue daily writing topics (page 41). Design your own spider's web lace (page 26). Do you have arachnophobia or know someone who does? Test your "fear factor" in the exercise on page 51.

2. Read and discuss the Anansi summary (page 20). Discuss how the West African stories arrived in Jamaica. Continue daily writing topics (page 41). Sequence the happenings in *Anansi, the Spider Man* (page 27). Discover why scorpions are called the living fossils (page 68).

3. Read and discuss the *Spider Weaver* summary (page 21). Continue daily writing topics (page 41). Answer the true or false questions about *The Spider Weaver* (page 28). Do the math mystery matchup (page 55).

4. Read and discuss the *Arachne* summary (page 20). Continue daily writing topics (page 41). Use your imagination to connect the dots and make your own constellation creations (page 25). For extra practice creating constellations, do the art project It's in the Stars (pages 70-71).

5. Read and discuss *Spider Woman* and *How Grandmother Spider Stole the Sun* summaries (page 22). Continue daily writing topics (page 41). Organize your students into a team to write their own version of *Spider Woman*. Do the exercise Team Writing: The Main Idea (page 29). Discuss scientific classification and do the exercise on page 60.

Extending the Book
---

1. Visit your local library during story hour. Encourage the librarian to have appropriate material for this section of our thematic unit. A good storyteller is a joy to hear.

2. Encourage your students to invite family members (especially ones who are good storytellers) into your classroom. Perhaps you could arrange to have a professional storyteller come.

3. Invite into your room any local artisans who can spin and/or use a loom. Ask your students how similar this weaving is to a spider's weaving. How difficult is it? How important is weaving in our lives? In the lives of people of the past? These are some questions you may wish to consider.

Constellation Creations

Ancient Greeks liked to gaze at the stars and try to detect figures in the sky (see It's in the Stars, page 70). Their process was somewhat like connecting dot-to-dot pictures. They saw the pattern below as Scorpius, the scorpion which stung Orion, the hunter, to death.

In the area below, create your own constellation for the same pattern, and then make up your own "myth" or "legend" for your creation on the back of this paper.

Spider's Web Lace

In the story of *The White Spider's Gift,* the spider makes a mantle of shimmering lace. It is full of beautiful designs of birds and flowers. Make your own designs on the mantle below. Remember that the ñandutí has a delicate beauty!

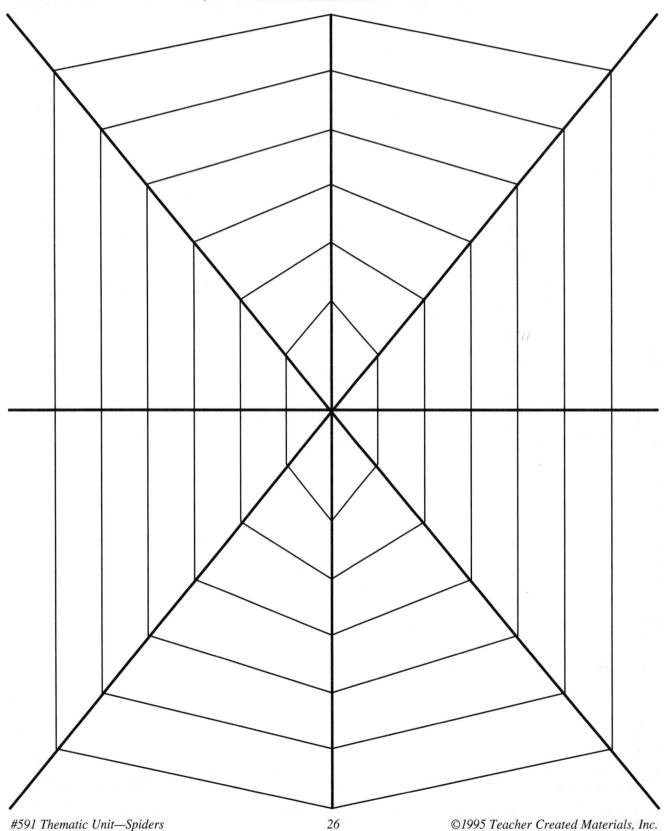

Sequencing *Anansi, the Spider Man*

Arrange the statements below in the correct order (from 1 to 10) just as they happened in our story of Anansi.

Incorrect Order

1. _____ Anansi tied up the foolish python.

2. _____ The Sky God gave Anansi his stories and called them Spider Stories.

3. _____ Anansi went to the Sky God to buy his stories.

4. _____ Anansi found a gourd that was the same size and shape as a hornet's nest.

5. _____ He fooled the hornets into thinking the rains had come.

6. _____ Anansi took the gourd of hornets to the Sky God.

7. _____ The Sky God wanted a python, a fairy, and 47 hornets for the stories.

8. _____ When 47 hornets flew into the gourd, Anansi put the plug in.

9. _____ The hornets flew into the gourd.

10. _____ Anansi captured a fairy with sticky sap and a doll.

Correct Order

1. _____

2. _____

3. _____

4. _____

5. _____

6. _____

7. _____

8. _____

9. _____

10. _____

True or False:
The Spider Weaver

A good deal of this tale is make-believe. There are some parts that could be true as we know them to be. For example, you know that there are farmers. Sort out which of the following statements are true (that is, could really happen) and which are false (or could never happen). Fill in the correct answer in the blanks next to each statement.

1. _____ A young farmer saves a spider from a snake which is about to eat it.
2. _____ A young girl can weave cloth.
3. _____ A spider weaves on a loom with its eight legs.
4. _____ The spider changes into a girl.
5. _____ A snake crawls into a bale of cotton.
6. _____ The spider eats the cotton.
7. _____ When the spider eats the cotton, she spins it into thread inside her body.
8. _____ The snake chases the spider again.
9. _____ The spider weaves clouds with cotton she ate.
10. _____ Clouds and spiders are called by the same name in Japan.

Now try your hand at creating five new actions that mix true (or real) conditions with impossible ones. Simply use the Spider Weaver tale as your basis and add new events that you make up. Be as imaginative as you wish.

1. _____

_____

2. _____

_____

3. _____

_____

4. _____

_____

5. _____

_____

Team Writing: The Main Idea

Here is a chance for you as a team to write your own version of the folk tale of *Spider Woman*. Below is a list of main ideas taken from the story of Spider Woman, Changing Woman, and her Twin Sons. To create a paragraph, each of you will add supporting details to one of the main ideas from the list. Use many descriptive words to make your paragraph interesting. You should use your imagination to develop the tale, but do not go beyond your main idea. You may wind up writing someone else's part if you do.

After everyone has finished writing, assemble into pairs. Read your paragraph to your partner. Have your partner ask questions and offer suggestions. Then change jobs. It becomes your turn to listen and to praise. After all the revisions are completed, read your complete story aloud. You may have your teacher read it first, and then each person can read his/her own paragraph for the second reading.

Paragraph Topics from *Spider Woman*

1. Changing Woman gave birth to twin sons.
2. The Sun was the father of Child Born of Water and Monster Slayer.
3. They grew up to be very strong hunters.
4. Changing Woman created the corn plant.
5. She mixed cornmeal with scrapings of her own skin to make the first Navajo people.
6. The Glittering World was filled with monsters and was unsafe for the Navajos.
7. The Twins set out to slay the monsters.
8. While hunting, the boys were called into a small hole in the ground.
9. The hole grew larger, they entered, and met Spider Woman.
10. Spider Woman helped the Twins to prepare for their dangerous journey.
11. Sharp reeds tried to cut them into pieces.
12. Sands tried to smother them.
13. Canyon tried to crush them.
14. Four rock columns had the power to turn them into old men.
15. The Great Snake, the Black Bear, the Big Thunder, and the Big Wind guarded the Sun's home. The Twins chanted prayers that Spider Woman taught them.
16. The Sun refused to admit that he was their father.
17. The Sun threw the boys against white spikes in the eastern wall.
18. The Sun threw the boys against yellow spikes in the western wall.
19. The Sun threw the boys against black spikes in the northern wall.
20. The Sun threw the boys against turquoise spikes in the southern wall.

Note to the teacher: Add, select, combine, or eliminate ideas as you wish to meet your class needs. Decide beforehand how many sentences each student should write. Remind them that they are only adding the supporting details, not writing the whole story.

Storytelling

Before humans learned to write about their lives and adventures, they shared their experiences by telling stories. People of all ages enjoy listening to storytellers. Tales have been told over and over again. Some parts are left out at times, and at other times parts are added. It is all left up to the storyteller and how much time is available for a story. This is how people have learned of their history. This is how the past is remembered.

As you can tell by the folk tales in this section, the art of storytelling is practiced all over the world. The ancient Greeks and Romans had their myths. The villages of Africa, South America, Jamaica, North America, Japan, and other places throughout the world have their storytellers. Now it is your chance to become a storyteller.

Use the story that you have written in team writing (page 29) or another one of your choice. Practice, practice, and practice reading aloud until you know your story by heart. Tell it to your friends, classmates, schoolmates, family, etc. Don't worry if it is not told word for word. Relax and have fun! It should be as if you are telling some tale about yourself or a family member. As a matter of fact, that is a good way to get practice in the art of storytelling. You are probably doing it already and don't realize that you are. You have been "sharing" since pre-school, haven't you? This is the same thing! For some specific help in preparing to be a really good storyteller, follow the advice given below.

Preparation for the Storyteller

1. Read your story aloud to yourself until every sentence sounds right—just the way you want it to sound.

2. When you are able to read it to your satisfaction in step one, try recording yourself on a tape cassette. (If you are able to videotape yourself, you may eliminate step six in this list.)

3. Listen to yourself on the cassette enough times so that you become familiar with your own voice. (At first, your own voice may sound strange to you.)

4. Make any voice-emphasis changes you think will improve your story, and tape-record yourself again.

5. Now that you know just how you want to tell the story, practice adding a few gestures to illustrate or emphasize your story.

6. Try telling the story in front of a mirror so you can both hear your voice and see your facial expressions and gestures.

7. Now you are ready for first-rate storytelling. Welcome to the wonderful world of storytelling—an ancient and completely enjoyable art.

Charlotte's Web
by E.B. White

Summary

Our story is not only a story about a spider named Charlotte A. Cavatica, but also the story of a very lucky pig. His name is Wilbur. How is he lucky? Well, first he is saved from death by the little girl Fern Arable. Wilbur is born a runt, small and weak. (On a farm a weakling makes trouble when one is raising a litter of pigs.) Fern talks her father into letting her have Wilbur. Fern does not think he is trouble. She enjoys bottle feeding him.

When Wilbur is five weeks old, he is sold to Fern's Uncle Homer. Fern is happy that Wilbur is still nearby so she can visit him. What Fern and Wilbur do not realize is that Homer Zuckerman is raising Wilbur to be butchered as food. That is what happens on farms. But Wilbur is lucky again. Charlotte comes into his life and weaves wonderful magic in her web. She not only helps control the balance of nature by capturing and eating pesky flies, but she also turns Wilbur into something grander than food on the table.

Charlotte begins to weave words into her web. Now Mr. Zuckerman and all the other gullible people think that Wilbur is "Terrific," "Some Pig," and "Radiant." Wilbur becomes Zuckerman's Famous Pig and travels to the county fair where he becomes "Humble," and Charlotte ends her life cycle. Before she does, she saves Wilbur and leaves her legacy in an egg sac, her "magnum opus." If you don't know Latin, you will have to read the book to discover its meaning.

Sample Plan

Day 1

- Read pages 1–31. Have SSR.
- Introduce daily writing topics (page 42).
- Find out where Charlotte is (page 34).
- Do the arachnid facts math exercise (page 56).

Day 2

- Read pages 32–65. Have SSR.
- Continue daily writing topics (page 42).
- Plot the answers (page 57).
- Find out about Charlotte's legs (page 35).

Day 3

- Read pages 66–104. Have SSR.
- Continue daily writing topics (page 42).
- Decide if Charlotte is bloodthirsty (page 36).
- Begin collecting spiders and webs (page 63).

Day 4

- Read pages 105–143. Have SSR.
- Continue daily writing topics (page 42).
- Discover carnival webs (page 37).
- Discover spiders in your neighborhood (page 65).

Day 5

- Read pages 144–184. Have SSR.
- Continue daily writing topics (page 42).
- Enjoy an edible-animals luncheon (page 38).
- Make your own starchy spider webs (page 69).

Overview of Activities

Setting the Stage

1. Introduce daily writing topics for *Charlotte's Web* (page 42).

2. Do some prior-knowledge idea webs about farm life, pigs, county fairs, etc.

3. Discuss the effect of giving names to creatures other than humans. Does this help us to relate to or better understand other creatures? What about the type of name? Are some names "friendly" and other names "scary"? Brainstorm a list of friendly names and scary names for creatures that are not soft, cuddly, furry, or usually regarded as pets by humans—for example, a squid, a bat, a worm, a lobster, an alligator, a piranha, or a cobra.

Enjoying the Book

1. Read and discuss pages 1–31. Ask your students if they have ever bottle-fed small animals. Ask them if they know what the capital of Pennsylvania is. Have any been on a farm, helped with chores, watched the animals? Continue daily writing topics (page 42). How observant are they? Can they find the single spider among all the insects in the game "Where's Charlotte?" (page 34). You may also wish to use the scene on page 34 as an exercise in listening and following directions. Do the arachnid facts math exercise (page 56).

2. Read and discuss pages 32–65. What type of spider is Charlotte? What type of web does she weave? What happens next? Continue daily writing topics (page 42). Find out about Charlotte's legs (page 35). This activity helps students learn about spiders and also teaches them about human anatomy. (It may surprise them to learn about some strong similarities between spider and human.) Plot the coordinates on page 57 to discover more spider facts. (While learning more about spiders, the students will also develop skill in graphing and reading coordinates for carry-over into math, map-reading, and science.)

3. Read and discuss pages 66–104. Ask why Charlotte thinks people are gullible. Why does a rotten egg explode when it breaks? Continue daily writing topics (page 42). Do you think Charlotte is bloodthirsty? Do the research and writing activities on page 36. Lead students to notice similarities in spider and human digestive systems. Begin collecting spiders and webs (page 63).

4. Read and discuss pages 105–143. Continue daily writing topics (page 42). Charlotte earlier talked about the Queensborough Bridge being a sort of web. (If we become interested in something, it is not uncommon to perceive similarities of form or structure in other things.) Discover carnival webs (page 37). Prepare a bulletin board with radiating spokes of yarn to simulate a Ferris wheel or merry-go-round. Use this as a display board for completed carnival web stories and poems. Pin the completed writing along and around the spokes of the carnival "web." Discover spiders in your neighborhood (page 65).

5. Read and discuss pages 144–184. Discuss Charlotte's "magnum opus" (page 144 in the selection). Extend the discussion to the use of this term for great works of art, music, and literature.

   Enjoy an edible-animals luncheon (page 38). Work on the art project to make starchy spider webs (page 69).

Overview of Activities *(cont.)*

Extending the Book

1. Have students list major characters that appear in our selection. Find a quote credited to each character. On a notecard, write the quote on one side and the character's name on the other.

   Example: "May I get a drink of milk? I think there are a few drops of milk left in my trough." (Wilbur)

   Break into small groups. Take turns reading your quotes. Let the others guess the characters. You can do the same thing using a sentence or two that describes the character.

   Example: "He wanted a friend, someone who would play with him." (Wilbur)

2. Have students list three things that they read about in our selection that they would like to learn more about. Have them list different sources where they might find the information. Decide whether they should research one or all of their listings.

3. Have students work in groups or by themselves to prepare questions and answers about possible future developments in the fiction parts of the story.

   Example:

   Q: What happens to Fern Arable? Does she still visit Wilbur every day?

   A: No, she spends a lot of time with Henry Fussy instead.

   There are many possible answers to that one question. (There are probably as many answers as you have students in your class, so accept reasonable questions and answers.)

4. Develop and present a reader's theater production for *Charlotte's Web*. This is an easy way to provide students the opportunity to perform a play without requiring elaborate props, sets, costumes or memorization. Students read the dialogue of the characters, narrator, etc., from the book or prepared script. The dialogue may be verbatim or with elaboration by the performer. By using several narrators and including the roles of Charlotte, Wilbur, Templeton, Old Sheep, Lurvy, Mr. Zuckerman, and Fern, many students can be involved with the activity. Other support activities involve script preparation, sound effects, greeting the audience, and preparation of invitations and props.

5. Perhaps an appropriate way to end this thematic unit is the way Charlotte's hatched children leave Wilbur—with a ballooning journey (page 74).

Where's Charlotte?

How are spiders our friends? All spiders are carnivorous. They feed primarily on insects. Many insects trapped by spiders are pests. That makes spiders invaluable to man and to the balance of nature. At certain times of the year, there may be as many as two million spiders in an acre of meadowland. Under ideal conditions, each may capture one small insect per day. That gets rid of a lot of insects. Add to the list other small insects, such as aphids, which become trapped in the webs of large spiders. Even if the spiders do not eat them, the insects usually do not escape the webs.

Look at the picture below. There are not two million spiders in this meadow. There is only one among all the insects. It's Charlotte! Can you find her?

Extension: If there are two million spiders in an acre of meadowland and each one eats one insect per day, how many is that in one week? One month? One year?

> **Note to the teacher:** Use this page for listening skills. Give students directions to circle or color certain insects or groups of insects, or other objects on the page. For example: Color three bees yellow; or color a red apple on the fence post to the left of the tree, etc.

Charlotte's Legs

While Wilbur is watching Charlotte repair her web, he can not help noticing her hairy legs. She tells him her legs are hairy for a good reason. She goes on to explain that each leg has seven sections. They are the coxa, the trochanter, the femur, the patella, the tibia, the metatarsus, and the tarsus.

The legs of spiders are very similar to those of insects. The legs are attached to the cephalothorax by the coxa (a short segment). The coxa is connected to another short segment called the trochanter. Next comes the femur, then the patella, the tibia, the metatarsus, and then the tarsus. The tarsus segment has either two or three claws attached to it. The legs of a spider are powered by sets of muscles running within the exoskeleton. These muscles flex and extend the leg sections in much the same way as in human beings.

The legs of humans are attached to the hip bone (pelvis). Next comes the femur (thigh bone). The femur is connected to the patella (knee cap). Then come the tibia (shin bone) and fibula which connect with the talus (ankle bone), then the tarsals, metatarsals, and phalanges (toe bones).

Using the information above (plus research if needed), label the bones on the two legs below.

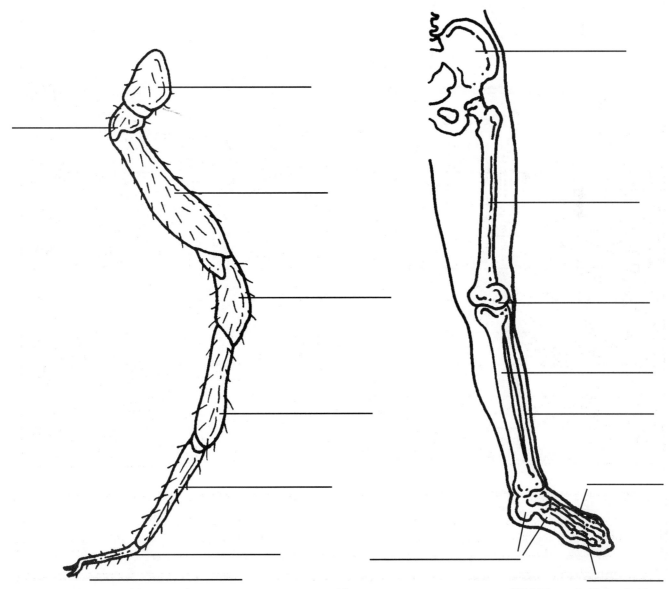

Bloodthirsty Charlotte?

When Charlotte and Wilbur are discussing eating flies, Wilbur is horrified to learn that Charlotte drinks them. She said: "Of course, I don't really eat them. I drink them—drink their blood. I love blood."

Wilbur thinks it is cruel and bloodthirsty. But Charlotte has to eat. Actually the spider's poison fangs and its pedipalps take the place of jaws. The spider does not actually chew with these "jaws." A spider's mouth is very small. Its food has to be so soft that the spider can suck it up. A spider can eat a great deal at one time. If it cannot catch any fresh food, it can live for a long time on the food it has stored in its body.

After poisoning a victim, a spider injects a fluid that predigests the tissue. The tissue then turns into a liquid the spider can suck into its stomach. It sometimes takes several hours for certain spiders to digest even a housefly. It is not just the blood that spiders drink, but all the soft parts. Then the hard shell is all that is left.

Now this may sound disgusting, but as Charlotte said, "I have to live, don't I?" If you know anything about the human digestive system, you know that it is not much different from the spider's. Our stomachs have juices that soften our food, but we do not have to poison our food first.

Research to find out just how similar our digestive systems are to those of spiders. Draw pictures or diagrams to accompany your short report. You may use the back of this page if needed.

Digestive Systems—Spiders and Humans

_____

_____

_____

_____

_____

_____

_____

_____

_____

_____

_____

Carnival Webs

Ferris wheels and merry-go-rounds are similar to an orb web. Can you name other carnival rides or other items that look like webs, such as bicycle wheels (spokes and hubs), etc.?

Now be fanciful and use your imagination. Pretend you are a giant spider and the Ferris wheel or merry-go-round is your web. Write a short story or poem to tell about you, your web, victims, etc.

After all stories and poems are completed, it is great fun to draw others into your web of story and poetry. Hold a read-around and share your creations.

Edible Animals

Have a little luncheon with Wilbur and Charlotte and enjoy some "edible animals" that the students make. Gather the materials. Decide beforehand what each student will bring. Some ideas are provided below. You may have some more of your own to add and use. The students, of course, can be very creative. Just give them the ingredients and see what they can construct.

Ingredients for Wilbur: boiled ham slices, cream cheese filling, olive slices, pretzel or breadstick stubs, red food coloring

Directions:

1. Make a cream cheese filling with softened cream cheese. Add (to taste) chopped olives, onions, garlic salt, and your own favorite ingredients. Add a little red food coloring to make a pink filling.

2. Spread some filling on a ham slice. Roll up the ham slice. Use a toothpick or pretzel stick to keep the shape. (Remember to keep a pig shape in mind.)

3. Place your pig on a slice of bread. Dip four pretzel or breadstick stubs into the filling to make them pink. Place in the appropriate places for legs. Use a smaller piece for his snout (nose/mouth) and ears. You can use olive slices for eyes. Don't worry if you smear the filling on your pieces. Just use a knife to touch up as best you can.

4. When you are ready to eat, remove toothpick (if used), roll up your filled ham creation in your slice of bread, and enjoy!

Wilbur's Trough:

Fill celery pieces with peanut butter, a veggie dip, or a cheese spread.

Ingredients for Charlotte: chocolate sandwich cookies (with double filling), large black gum drop, black candy laces, white gel cake decorating tubes, frosting (optional).

Directions:

1. Attach the gumdrop (stomach) to the sandwich cookie (cephalothorax) with a toothpick or some frosting to make it stick.

2. Add black candy laces for legs (8); pedipalps (2); spinnerets (on the stomach).

3. Use the gel to make eyes (2–8).

Want more ideas for barnyard animals? How about cheeseball chicks on a cracker? Cauliflower/cream cheese molded to make sheep? Marshmallow geese? Let your imagination go wild! Give your taste buds a treat! Have fun!

Writer's Workbook

Every student should have a notebook and a folder with his/her name on each. Title it appropriately for this thematic unit. Students should use this notebook to record ideas, take notes, write assignments from the daily writing topics, etc. In the folder, they can keep track of any handouts you may give them.

Keeping notes is a good way to remember important information.

Use clue words to remember a larger text—either a whole idea or just a sentence.

- arachnids—a group of animals to which spiders belong
- spiderling—young spiders

This is an example of condensing information. In a text that has a lot of information, you can make your own glossary to help remember the terms you are reading about. Record this information in your notebook (Writer's Workbook).

While reading *Charlotte's Web*, take notes while reading each section. Here are some ideas to note.

1. List characters as they appear in each section. Write descriptions.

2. Note the setting or settings of each section.

3. Note important events as they happen.

4. Note major changes that occur in characters or settings.

5. Note problems or goals that occur and/or are solved.

6. Note page and paragraph where word bank words are found, along with definitions.

At first, taking notes while reading will slow the readers down. So allow ample time to finish each reading selection. Plan to go over the notes after the reading is completed, during group discussion time. This will give the students an opportunity to understand the best way to consolidate their activities and condense their information. The extra time you take in the beginning will be harvested as your students become more aware of the material they are reading. By the time you get to the last section, the students should understand what you expect of them.

Take some time to evaluate their workbook entries. Nonjudgmental responses will please and encourage the students to write more. Remind your students that inventive spelling is acceptable while taking notes. Also, incomplete sentences will suffice.

Daily Writing Topics

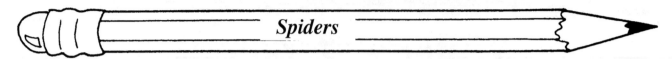

Spiders

1. Write a report on the different parts of a spider and their functions.

2. Make a list of the different types of webs that spiders weave.

3. Choose a web type. Describe how it is built and its function.

4. Write a comparison of how a garden spider and a crab spider catch their food.

5. Write a report about parasites that are enemies of spiders.

6. Write a report about spider wasps.

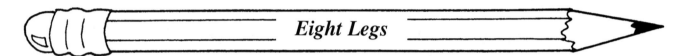

Eight Legs

1. Write a report on the differences between arachnids and insects.

2. Write an article on the eyes of spiders. Tell why you think some have 8, 6, 4, or 2.

3. Pretend you are an eye specialist. Write a report on your development of glasses for near-sighted spiders. Include illustrations.

4. Explain the molting process you are familiar with (human, animal, insect, etc.). Emphasize metamorphosis.

5. Choose an arachnid to write a report on. Include birth, habitat, prey, enemies, and life span.

6. Write an instruction manual on how to weave an orb web. Include illustrations and step-by-step procedures.

7. Explain in a paragraph the purpose of ballooning.

8. Explain the differences between web weavers and hunters. List pros and cons.

9. Do some spiders raise their babies? Explain your answer in a paragraph.

10. Write an interview with someone who has been bitten by a black widow spider (fact or fiction).

11. Use your imagination to interview Orion, the hunter, from the Greek myth. Interview him before he is bitten by the scorpion. Then interview him shortly after.

12. Interview the scorpion-goddess Selquet of Ancient Egypt. Find out why she chose the scorpion as her symbol.

13. Write a report on the similarities and differences between mites and ticks.

40

Daily Writing Topics *(cont.)*

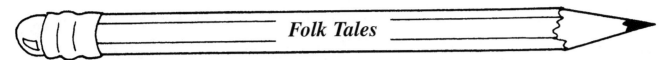

Folk Tales

1. Pretend you are a reporter interviewing the Indian boy who rescued the tiny white spider from drowning. Get a first-hand report from him. (You might want to make sure to ask why he did it and what happened because of it.)

2. Pretend you are a society editor. Write a story about the wedding. Interview the bride.

3. Interview the two old women who stole Spider's bag of thread. Find out why they did it and how they got the idea for a poncho.

4. Pretend you are Anansi, the Spider Man. Write an entry in your diary after you visit with the Sky God.

5. Pretend you are the Sky God. Write a letter to another god and tell him how Anansi got your stories.

6. Write a story for an arts and crafts magazine about the spider weaver.

7. Interview the farmer and have him describe how it looked to see the spider making clouds.

8. Write a short conversation between Arachne and Athena.

9. Write a short conversation between Athena and another goddess discussing what Athena did to Arachne.

10. Interview the twins of Changing Woman. Find out about their encounter with Spider Woman.

11. Pretend you are one of the twins. Write a letter to your brother years after your adventure. Reminisce about your experiences.

12. Imagine you are the Sun. Write a diary entry about the dangerous tests the Twins went through successfully.

13. Interview Changing Woman to find out what she thinks of Spider Woman and the Twins' escapade.

14. Imagine you are the Fox. Tell about your attempt to steal a piece of the sun.

15. Imagine you are the Possum. Tell about your attempt to steal a piece of the sun.

16. Imagine you are Grandmother Spider. Tell about your attempt to steal a piece of the sun.

17. Imagine you are the Buzzard. Tell about your determination to take the sun to the top of the sky.

18. Interview Grandmother Spider. Find out how she feels about the honors given her.

Daily Writing Topics *(cont.)*

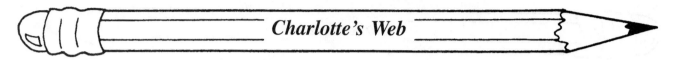

Charlotte's Web

1. Imagine you are Fern. Write a diary entry about saving Wilbur from an untimely death.

2. Pretend you are Fern's teacher. Write a note to Fern's parents, explaining her strange behavior. Don't forget to mention Fern's statement that the capital of Pennsylvania was "Wilbur."

3. Write five diary entries for each of the five weeks that Fern cares for Wilbur at her home.

4. Pretend you are Wilbur. Write an account of your first day in the manure pile in the cellar of Zuckerman's barn.

5. Write a diary entry for Fern after a visit with Wilbur at the barn.

6. Pretend you are Mrs. Zuckerman. Write a letter to a friend. Tell about the day the pig got out.

7. Write a song about Wilbur's loneliness.

8. Interview the goose. Get her description of Charlotte's and Wilbur's first meeting.

9. Pretend you are Wilbur. Write a journal entry about Charlotte's diet.

10. Interview Templeton. Get his view of life in the barn cellar.

11. Write an account of a conversation between Mrs. Arable and Dr. Dorian as they discuss Fern and the animals she talks to.

12. Write an account from Templeton's viewpoint of Wilbur's attempt to spin a web. From Charlotte's viewpoint.

13. Interview Charlotte. Find out why she thinks people are not as smart as bugs.

14. Pretend you are Avery. Write a paragraph about the swing in Zuckerman's barn.

15. Interview the minister to get his opinion on the miracle in Zuckerman's barn cellar.

16. Research to find out what St. Vitus's Dance is. Write a paragraph about it.

17. Interview Lurvy to find out how he feels about this terrific pig.

18. Pretend you are the reporter on the *Weekly Chronicle*. Write a story about "Zuckerman's Famous Pig."

19. Pick one of the people or creatures that went to the fair. Write an account of the happenings from that person's or creature's viewpoint.

20. Write a diary entry in Henry Fussy's diary after the fair is over.

21. Write an account of the food at the fair from Templeton's point of view.

22. Write an account of Avery being a clown in a ring at the fair.

23. Write an account of Wilbur's appreciation of Charlotte's friendship.

24. Describe your favorite event of the book. Tell why you like it.

Making Books

Have students make books using various suggestions throughout the unit. You can use the ideas in the daily writing topics or the word bank terms.

Parts of a Book

1. **Front Cover:** includes book title, author's name, illustration, and illustrator's name (Example: *Spiders—Our Friends* by Ms. Bonkrude's Room.)

2. **Title Page:** includes book title, author, illustrator, and publishing company

3. **Dedication Page:** honors one or more special people

4. **Table of Contents:** lists what is inside the book by subject or by authors

5. **Author Page:** describes the author and may include the author's family background, hobbies, and other books written by the author

6. **Back Cover:** may include an illustration and book reviews from magazines, book clubs, newspapers, etc

On this page and the next few, there are several book-making methods. Select one appropriate for your book topic.

Big Books

Purchase blank books at teacher supply stores or make your own.

Materials: tagboard or heavy paper, metal rings, hole reinforcers, crayons, colored pencils or markers, scissors, glue.

Directions:

Have students make book pages from sheets of tagboard.

- Punch three holes on the left hand side of each sheet of tagboard. Cover the front and back of each hole with reinforcers.

- Connect all pages with metal rings.

- These books may be shared with other students and displayed in the class along with other unit-related materials.

Making Books *(cont.)*

Shape Books

Materials: construction paper, tagboard, or heavy paper; crayons, colored pencils, or markers; pencil; scissors; stapler

Directions:

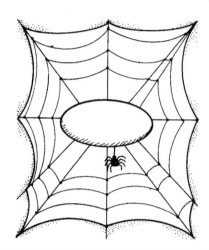

- Have students trace (or use the copy machine to produce) enough copies of the spider web pattern on page 45 to use as book pages.

- Provide each student with a copy of the pattern, as is, for the cover.

- Have students write sentences and do illustrations on each page. Combine the finished pages and staple them together along one edge.

Wheel Books

Materials: Construction paper or tagboard, scissors, crayons or colored pencils, brads, pencil

Directions:

- Make copies of the patterns on pages 46–47.

- Have students cut out the wheel pattern, the spider, and the dashed windows on the spider's abdomen.

- Help students attach the center of the wheel behind the spider with a brad.

- Direct students to color their covers. Have students draw a picture in the wheel section on the right side of the cover. In the wheel section on the left side of the spider, have students write a sentence or a word describing the picture.

- Help students turn their wheels and repeat this procedure until all wheel sections are completed. There should be four written sections and four picture sections.

44

Shape Book Pattern

Wheel Book Pattern

46

Wheel Book Pattern *(cont.)*

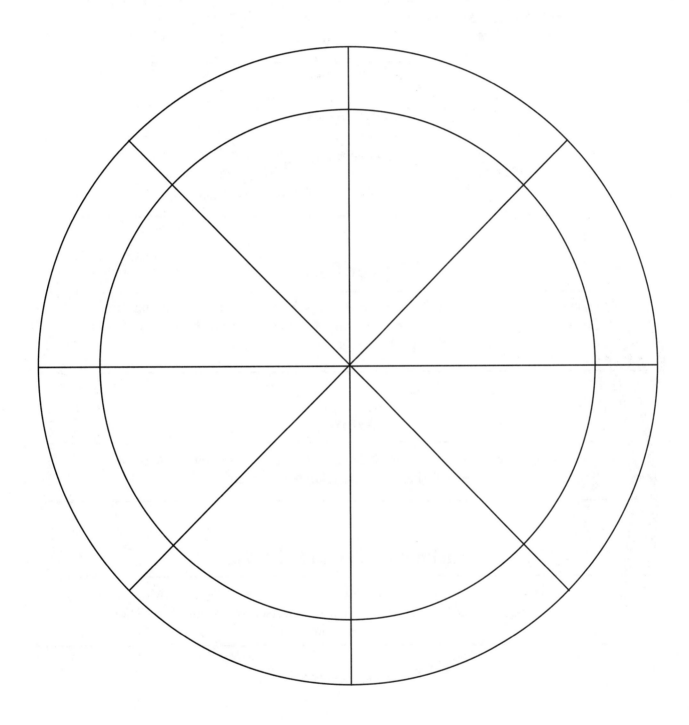

Word Bank

Spiders

black widow ✻ garden ✻ crab ✻ jumping wolf ✻ zebra ✻ huntsman ✻ orb weaver
nursery web ✻ fishing ✻ grass ✻ trap door ✻ purse web ✻ comb-footed ✻ tarantula
American house ✻ barn ✻ bolas ✻ lynx ✻ brown recluse ✻ cave ✻ flower
funnel web ✻ golden silk ✻ monkey ✻ sheet web weavers ✻ water

Arachnids

harvestmen (daddy longlegs) ✻ scorpion ✻ whipscorpion ✻ windscorpion ✻ mite
harvestmen mites ✻ spider mites ✻ velvet mites ✻ chigger ✻ water mites ✻ ticks
wood tick ✻ deer tick ✻ bear tick

Spider Parts

cephalothorax ✻ chelicerae ✻ carapace ✻ fangs ✻ eyes ✻ abdomen ✻ spinnerets
pedipalp ✻ legs ✻ poison ducts ✻ book lung ✻ setae ✻ venom ✻ spiracles ✻ silk
cuticles ✻ eggs ✻ egg sacs ✻ sucking stomach

Webs

orb ✻ triangle ✻ funnel ✻ bowl ✻ hammock ✻ dome ✻ cobwebs ✻ purse
✻ bell-shaped ✻ irregular ✻ bola web

Arachnologists and Scientists

Jean Lamarck ✻ Carolus Linnaeus ✻ Edwin Way Teale ✻ J. Traherne Moggridge
Jean Henri Fabre ✻ William Beebe ✻ Willis J. Gertsch ✻ Raymond W. Thorp
B.J. Kaston

Crossword Puzzle

To acquaint yourself with names and terms that will be used throughout this thematic unit, complete the crossword puzzle below. All words used in the puzzle appear in the word bank above the puzzle.

Word Bank

abdomen ✳ cephalothorax ✳ chelicerae ✳ cobweb ✳ eggs ✳ fang ✳ orb ✳ pedipalp
recluse ✳ silk ✳ spinnerets ✳ venom ✳ widow ✳ wolf ✳ zebra

Across:

2. the front section of a spider's body

5. leglike structures on side of mouth

6. "The Black_____ Spider" (a movie)

8. a round-shaped web

9. openings where silk threads leave body

11. part of the jaw that has poison ducts

12. the brown _____ , a poisonous spider

13. a poisonous liquid

Down:

1. a web that has an irregular shape

2. the jaws of a spider

3. back section of a spider's body

4. a striped jumping spider

7. a hunting spider with big eyes

9. thread produced in spider's body

10. a spider may lay 1,000 of these

Arachnid Word Search

Find the names of some arachnids hidden in the puzzle below. You will find them vertically, horizontally, and diagonally. Circle them as you find them. The words are listed below in the word bank.

Word Bank

black widow ✱ chigger ✱ crab spider ✱ daddy longlegs ✱ fishing spider ✱ garden spider
harvestmen ✱ harvestmite ✱ house spider ✱ scorpion ✱ spider mite ✱ tarantulas
velvet mite ✱ whip scorpion ✱ wood tick

```
G A R D E N S P I D E R C X Y F Z
D W O O O D T I K C E R H A V I B
A S P I D S P I D E R M I T E S C
D S C O R P I O N E S T G Q L H L
D H A R V E S T M E N N G Q V I H
Y T A R A N T U L A S E E R E N I
L B W H I B L A C K T A R E T G T
O A H I P U S P M I T E H C M S G
N C I H N U M P M I T E O L I P M
G K P W O O D T I C K Z U U T I I
L S N O B X S I T D A D D Y E D N
E P S O O E H O U S E S P I D E R
G I O D V E S T S P I R D E R R T
S C T R P I O N A B D O M E A L S
A R A V E L V E C R A B H O U S P
W H I P S C O R P I O N L I S P Y
C H I G G B L A C K W I D O W I D
V E L V E T S C O R P I N A R T R
```

Arachnophobia: Fear Factors

Arachnophobia (ah rak nih FOE bee uh) is an extraordinary fear of spiders and other arachnids. People have been deathly afraid of them, so afraid that they panic everytime they see one. They may run away, scream, faint, or behave in other wild and strange ways!

Do you remember this nursery rhyme?

> Little Miss Muffett
> Sat on a tuffet,
> Eating her curds and whey.
> Along came a spider
> Who sat down beside her,
> And frightened Miss Muffett away!

Do you suppose little Miss Muffett suffered from arachnophobia?

The tarantula is among the largest of all spiders. It is hairy and fierce looking. The venom of the North American tarantula is quite mild; no known deaths have resulted from its bite (although the South American tarantula can be quite dangerous). But in the past (and maybe even today) people have been scared to death! If you saw the movie *Home Alone*, perhaps you will remember how frightened one of the bad guys got when a pet tarantula walked across him. There was also a movie called *Arachnophobia*. Those nasty spiders in the movie scared many—just as was intended.

During the Middle Ages in Europe, the fear of the tarantula was even worse than it is now. Many people believed that the tarantula's venom was very powerful and that it made people dance about wildly! Because people believed this (the power of suggestion?) they danced madly around when bitten. They would spin around and jump up and down without stop or rest. They would do this for hours or even whole days until they collapsed from exhaustion. Some recovered but others died, victims of their fear of spiders—arachnophobia!

Do you have arachnophobia? In this activity, you can rate your fear factor. You must defend your ratings by using evidence from the reading selections and/or life experiences.

Note to the teacher: Copy the following statements on the board or overhead projector. Choose one of the arachnids from the word bank (page 48). Insert the word in each blank. Have students choose a number from the ratings that best fits their fear factor. They must be prepared to support their ratings. After you work together as a class, allow the students to complete the ratings individually for the rest of the arachnids or any number you choose.

1. _____ are something I fear little _____ greatly.
                                                                     1   2   3   4   5

2. _____ are never _____ often found near my home.
                                                       1   2   3   4   5

3. _____ habitats are not very _____ very noticeable.
                                                       1   2   3   4   5

4. Deaths from _____ occur rarely _____ always.
                                                           1   2   3   4   5

Homonym "Cents" About Tarantulas

A homonym is a word that sounds the same as another word but is spelled differently and has another meaning. In the short article below are some misused homonyms. See if you can find them. Need a clue? A blank is provided next to a sentence that contains the misspelled word. Write the word correctly on the blank.

Naturalists are continuing to learn about the

1. _____ tarantula's senses. They do no that the spider has

2. _____ ate eyes. They're located just above its mouth. It

3. _____ doesn't seam as if it's enough, though, because it

4. _____ can't sea objects more than a few inches away. A

5. _____ grasshopper can bee sitting still just a foot away,

6. _____ and the tarantula won't know it's their.

7. _____ Inn order to hunt, the tarantula needs to depend on

8. _____ its well-developed cents of touch. The body hairs

9. _____ (setae) act as sensors two sense movement and vibration.

10. _____ At times, an insect gets away. It doesn't become pray

11. _____ if it can stay very still. Sum naturalists think

these big spiders have a good sense of taste and smell.

12. _____ Caged tarantulas won't eat some insects oar cockroaches

that don't taste good. These spiders don't have noses, but

they do have odor detectors. They are white lyre organs on the

underside of their legs. During

13. _____ the mating season, mails can detect a female's

14. _____ cent from a mile (1.6 km) or more away.

Extension: List below other homonyms that you can think of.

Triangle Web Addition

What is the triangle spider about to catch in her triangle web? Look for the addition pattern and complete the triangle web by placing the appropriate number in each space. Then place the proper letter in the blanks below.

What is H. cavatus having for lunch?

___ ___ ___ ___ ___ ___ ___ ___ ___ ___ ___
135   27   7   11   11   2   38   73   73   47   27

Spider/Web Math Matchup

These Araneus spiders have lost their webs. You know how nearsighted they are! Attach a dragline to each spider's spinneret and connect them with the proper web. How will you know which web belongs with each A. diadematus? Solve the problems on the webs and on the spiders. Find and connect the matches.

Extension: What is the name the A. diadematus is usually known as (A.K.A.)?

Mystery Match

To discover the Mystery Word, draw a line to connect the dots by each problem in the left-hand column with the problem in the right-hand column that has the same total. Then write the letters that are intersected by a line in the order they are found from left to right and top to bottom.

Mystery Word: _____

1. 3x8	= _____ •	• 90÷5 = _____
2. 3x6	= _____ •	• 6x4 = _____
3. 4x7	= _____ •	• 15+21 = _____
4. 4x9	= _____ •	• 143-115 = _____
5. 5x8	= _____ •	• 120÷3 = _____
6. 6x7	= _____ •	• 35+13 = _____
7. 6x8	= _____ •	• 21x2 = _____
8. 6x9	= _____ •	• 75-21 = _____
9. 7x7	= _____ •	• 21x3 = _____
10. 7x8	= _____ •	• 98÷2 = _____
11. 7x9	= _____ •	• 33+23 = _____
12. 8x4	= _____ •	• 141-109 = _____
13. 8x8	= _____ •	• 380-299 = _____
14. 8x9	= _____ •	• 50+50-100 = _____
15. 9x9	= _____ •	• 25x4 = _____
16. 10x0	= _____ •	• 136-72 = _____
17. 10x10	= _____ •	• 6x2 = _____
18. 100x10	= _____ •	• 72x1 = _____
19. 11x2	= _____ •	• 66÷3 = _____
20. 12x1	= _____ •	• 999+1 = _____

Letters (center):

S   A
P
R
A
I
C
D   H
N
O
P
E   H
O   B
I
R
A
S

Extension: Unscramble the unused letters to discover what the mystery word does NOT like.

Arachnid Facts

Solve each problem below. Then write the answer in the blank to find out some interesting facts about arachnids.

1. 2,000x20 = _____ . There are more than _____ kinds of spiders found throughout the world.

2. 96÷12 = _____. A spider has _____ legs.

3. 2x0 = _____. A spider has _____ wings.

4. 960–957 = _____. Little spiders have been discovered "ballooning" nearly _____ miles above the earth's surface.

5. 1+0 = _____. A common garden spider can spin a web that is 3–4 feet (1–1.3 meters) across in _____ hour.

6. 5x5 = _____. A purse web spider will build a nest that may be up to 10 inches (_____ centimeters) or more in length.

7. 45÷3 = _____. The venom of a black widow spider is _____ times more powerful than that of a rattlesnake.

8. (1÷4)+(1÷4) = _____. The black widow spider is black and shiny all over. It is about _____ inch long.

9. 3,347–1,347 = _____. About _____ people are bitten by black widow spiders every year in the U.S.

10. 5x2 = _____. About _____ people die as a result of these bites.

11. 250x4 = _____. A black widow spider may lay as many as _____ eggs.

12. 800÷2 = _____. Scorpions have been around for almost _____ million years.

13. 231+469 = _____. The order Scorpionida is made up of six families, which include _____ or more kinds of scorpions known in the world.

14. 40x5 = _____. There are about _____ species of harvestmen in North America.

15. 400x50 = _____. More than _____ species of mites are named, probably a fraction of the total.

Plot the Answers

Learn some facts about spiders and other arachnids by plotting the answers. Find the coordinates on the grid. Then write the letter that is in that space on the proper lines below. (The bottom coordinate goes first.)

4	S	N	E	Z	B	V	F	I	L
3	D	R	O	H	U	M	I	G	Y
2	N	X	A	W	J	T	O	A	E
1	I	Q	U	P	E	A	K	C	U
0	1	2	3	4	5	6	7	8	9

1. Spiders are members of the phylum ___ ___ ___ ___ ___ ___ ___ ___ ___ , a large
   3,2 2,3 6,2 4,3 3,3 4,1 7,2 1,3 8,2
   group of animals with jointed legs and a hard outer skeleton.

2. They belong to the class ___ ___ ___ ___ ___ ___ ___ ___ ___ which includes
   6,1 2,3 8,2 8,1 4,3 1,2 1,1 1,3 3,2
   animals with four pairs of legs, no antennae or wings, and only two main body parts.

3. The two body parts are the abdomen and the ___ ___ ___ ___ ___ ___ ___ ___ ___ ___ ___ ___ ___ .
   8,1 5,1 4,1 4,3 3,2 9,4 3,3 6,2 4,3 7,2 2,3 8,2 2,2.

4. The cephalothorax contains the ___ ___ ___ ___ ___ , poison glands, and stomach.
   5,4 2,3 3,2 7,3 2,4

5. In the abdomen are the heart, digestive tract, reproductive organs, lungs and respiratory tracheae,
   and ___ ___ ___ ___ ___ ___ ___ ___ ___ ___ .
   1,4 8,4 9,4 7,1 8,3 9,4 8,2 2,4 1,3 1,4.

6. ___ ___ ___ ___ ___ ___ ___ ___ ___ ___ (usually 6) issue strands of silk through tiny spigots.
   1,4 4,1 1,1 2,4 1,2 9,2 2,3 5,1 6,2 1,4

7. ___ ___ ___ ___ ___ ___ ___ ___ ___ by the adult male spider begins after his palp is filled
   8,1 3,3 3,1 2,3 6,2 1,4 4,3 7,3 4,1
   with sperm and he has found a female.

8. Males usually ___ ___ ___ soon after mating.
   1,3 1,1 5,1

9. Most spiders make silken ___ ___ ___ cases.
   9,2 8,3 8,3

10. Growth of a spider requires shedding its ___ ___ ___ ___ ___ ___ ___ ___ ___ ___ ___
    9,2 2,2 3,3 1,4 7,1 5,1 9,4 9,2 6,2 7,2 2,4
    usually 4-12 times before maturity.

11. Most spiders live 1 or 2 seasons. Some___ ___ ___ ___ ___ ___ ___ may live up to 20 years.
    7,4 9,2 6,3 3,2 9,4 3,4 1,4

12. The largest scorpion grows well over ___ ___ ___ inches long. Tarantulas are the biggest
    1,4 8,4 2,2
    spiders. One species has a 3 ½ inch (9 cm) body with a leg span of 10 inches (25 cm).

Bar Graph

Spider	Average Length
1. Tarantula	90 mm
2. Trap door spider	30 mm
3. Funnel web mygalomorph	50mm
4. Spitting spider	8 mm
5. Purse web spider	30 mm
6. Black widow	32 mm
7. Nephila	25 mm
8. American house spider	8 mm
9. Dwarf spider	2 mm
10. Garden spider	11 mm

Complete the bar graph below to show the average length of each spider listed in the chart above.

Remember: 10 mm = 1 cm

S P I D E R S

1.
2.
3.
4.
5.
6.
7.
8.
9.
10.

0   10   20   30   40   50   60   70   80   90   10

millimeters

Length in ~~Centimeters~~ (cm)

Answer the following questions using the bar graph and chart for your data.

1. Which spider is the longest? _____

2. Which spider is the smallest? _____

3. How many ~~centimeters~~ *mm* long is the Nephila? _____

4. Which two spiders are ~~three cm~~ *30 mm* long? _____

5. How much longer is the tarantula than the funnel web mygalomorph? _____

6. Which two spiders together are half as long as the black widow? _____

Use < (smaller than) or > (greater than) to compare spider lengths.

7. trap-door _____ spitting

8. dwarf _____ black widow

9. garden _____ nephila

10. funnel web _____ purse web

Science

Scientific Classification

Common Names and Scientific Names

Did you know that every spider has a scientific name? Not every spider, however, has a common name. And when a spider does have a common name, it may not be called by that name everywhere in the world. What we call a black widow spider, someone in Mexico calls "arana capulina," or cherry spider. In Russia it is called a "black wolf spider." In South Africa, it is called "shoe button spider." New Zealanders refer to the widow as the "night stinger." In Australia, they call it the "red-black spider." How do scientists know which kind of widow spider you are talking about? The answer to that question is that all animals (and plants) are given scientific names.

Species

Scientific names are part of the system of classification which is used all over the world by all scientists. With this classification, scientists can show how different plants and animals are related to each other. Animals that are similar are grouped together and given the same scientific name. We say that they belong to the same *species*. Human beings are a species and have been given the species name Homo sapiens. An animal's name is made up of two words in Latin or Greek. The common species of black widow spiders found in the southern states is called Latrodectus mactans. Another type found in the western part of the U.S. that has the red hourglass marking but not olive-gray or pink markings is called Latrodectus hesperus.

Genus

The next group in scientific classification is the *genus*. A genus is made up of more than one species. Animals that belong to the same genus are closely related but are not as much alike as the members of the same species. The black bear belongs to the genus Ursus. Its species name is Ursus americanus. There are other types of bears that belong to the same genus. The grizzly bear species name is Ursus arctos. For many years it was classed as Ursus horribilis, but most authorities now use that term to classify the difference between grizzlies (Ursus arctos horribilis) and the Kodiak bear, Ursus arctos middendorffi. These types of classifications are called subspecies. The polar bear is known as Ursus maritimus among scientists. The giant panda bear is known as Ailuropoda melanoleuca. What does that tell you about the giant panda bear? (Hint: If neither the genus nor species name is the same as those of other bears, can these animals be very closely related?) Some scientists, in fact, think this animal does not even belong in the bear family, placing it instead in the raccoon family. (Now see what you can learn about the koala bear.)

Family

Just as a genus is made up of several species, a *family* is made up of more than one genus. They are similar but with some important differences. Lions, leopards, tigers, and domestic cats belong to the family Felidae. Dogs, foxes, coyotes, and wolves belong to the family Canidae. Bears belong to the family Ursidae. All black widow spiders belong to the family Theridiidae, the comb-footed spiders.

Scientific Classification *(cont.)*

Order, Class, Phylum, Kingdom

Families of animals are parts of even larger groups—order, class, phylum, and kingdom—in the system of classification. In the 18th century, a Swede by the name of Carolus Linnaeus developed a structured form of biological classification. Below is an example of a black widow spider and how it fits into this system of biological classification.

- Kingdom: Animalia
- Phylum: Arthropoda
- Class: Arachnida
- Order: Araneae
- Family: Theridiidae
- Genus: Latrodectus
- Specific Name: mactans

This system is a useful tool both for scientists and for people who want to learn about the world of nature. The majority of spiders lack common names. Since there are more than 40,000 different kinds, many are known only by their scientific names.

Word Bank

Canidae ✳ classification ✳ family ✳ Felidae ✳ genus ✳ Homo sapiens ✳ Latrodectus
mactans ✳ Carolus Linnaeus ✳ species ✳ Ursus americanus

Find each word from the word bank in the above article. Using colored pencils, underline each word with a different color. Then with the same color, for each word, underline its definition.

Extension: Using the Scientific Classification and Identification Form (page 61), practice identifying some of the spiders you have been studying or any other animal you may choose. Use guides, field guides, books, and encyclopedias to get the information you will need. Draw pictures or cut them out of magazines or write complete descriptions of the animal you choose. Then by means of a map or written description, identify the habitat (the region where an animal naturally lives).

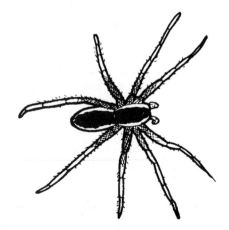

Scientific Classification ID Form

_____

Animal

- Kingdom:

- Phylum:

- Class:

- Order:

- Family:

- Genus:

- Specific Name:

Picture or description	Habitat

Scientific Crossword Puzzle

Complete this crossword puzzle about arachnids, using the words from the word bank below. You will need to experiment to find where the remaining words will fit. (Hint: The numbers 1-8 occur in order horizontally from top to bottom and left to right.)

Word Bank

chigger ✳ eight ✳ harvestmen ✳ insects ✳ mite ✳ scorpion ✳ spider tick

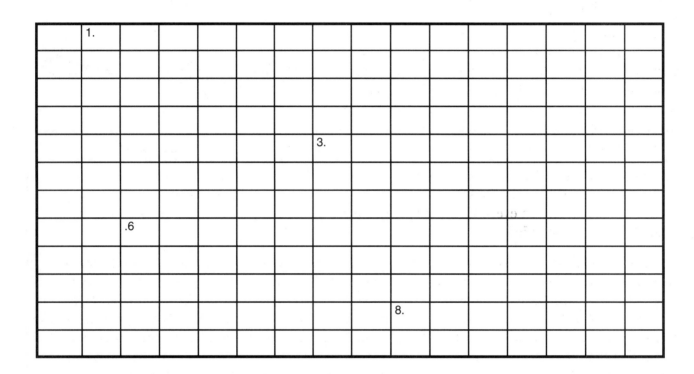

Across

1.

5.   It has pincers and a long tail with a stinger at its tip.

6.

7.   How many legs does a spider have?

8.

Down

2.   Another name for daddy longlegs.

3.

4.   An arachnid's favorite meal (plural).

Now write clues in their proper place for those words that have been provided.

Collecting Spiders and Webs

Spiders are found nearly everywhere, thank goodness! You will find them in houses, gardens, fields, woods, and under bark, stones, leaves, or logs. (Remember to replace any stones or logs you may move, so the habitat is not destroyed after you have searched.) There are many different methods you can use to collect spiders. The type of spider you collect will determine the equipment to use. Some suggestions appear in the following paragraphs.

Spiders that run along the ground can be chased into a can or simply picked up if you are not squeamish. Capture spiders in shrubs and herbs with an insect net. You can make a metal can trap by burying a can flush with the ground surface. Put some anti-freeze (ethylene glycol) in the bottom. On stones above the buried can, place bark or some wood for a lid to keep out the rain. Don't forget to take the can out when you are finished collecting. Using a flashlight or a miner's headlamp, try collecting at night. Wolf spiders, with their large eyes, will reflect light. You can also find some orb weavers in their webs at night.

As you collect the spiders, drop them in a vial of alcohol, either 80% grain alcohol or 70–80% isopropyl (rubbing) alcohol. Because of their soft bodies, spiders cannot be pinned and dried like insects. Attach a label to every vial. On the label include the date, location, habitat, the name of the spider (when it is identified), and your name.

If you wish to keep live spiders, a terrarium will be a good container. You must consider the size of your spider when choosing a terrarium. Tarantulas, of course, will need a large container. A five-gallon fish tank with aquarium gravel in the bottom makes a good terrarium. Do not use dirt from your yard, as it may carry parasites. Some pet stores sell tarantulas. They can advise you on the best way to care for your pet. Remember to put a lid on the container because tarantulas can climb up glass walls. Remember that they need to breathe. They also need to be kept warm. Use large rocks to make a burrow. You will need a small container for a water dish. Tarantulas are insect eaters. Almost any insect you can catch, they will eat. Pet stores will have crickets or mealy worms to feed them in the winter if you cannot find any insects. Tarantulas never overeat, and they often go weeks without food during the winter.

If you want to keep a burrowing spider, try digging the burrow and all! Place the spider and all materials carefully in a gallon jar with a screen on it for a lid. Web-weaving spiders can be kept in wooden frames with glass or plastic sides. Each spider needs its own space, or it will eat the other.

To collect webs, use a glass frame and a dark background such as cardboard or tagboard. When you find a web to collect, place the background on one side of the web, the glass frame on the other. Sandwich the web between them and clip the excess with scissors.

Widow Spiders Around the World

There are many different species of widow spiders in many areas of the world. Their scientific name, or genus (see pages 59–60), means "a biting robber."

On the map below, color in the areas where widow spiders can be found. Use an encyclopedia or some of the books listed in the bibliography (page 77) to find out information on their habitat.

Extension: Use different colors to indicate different species of widow spiders. Don't forget to make a key to explain your information.

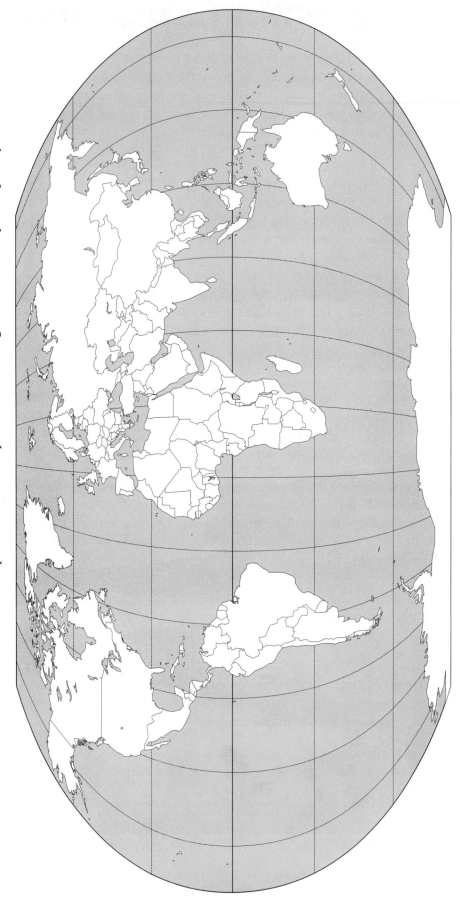

Spiders in Our Neighborhood

Spiders are found in widely varied places from the equator to the far north. They have been found above the tree line on Mount Everest, and they have been found at the bottoms of ponds. Ballooning spiderlings have been seen hundreds of miles out to sea and nearly three miles above the earth's surface. Where have you found spiders in your neighborhood? You can find them inside and outside. In rural areas, large cities, and small towns, you will find an array of spiders searching for insects in their own ways. They will be on the ground, floor, wall, tree, bush, table, flower, chair, or almost any place you care to look.

Select an area to investigate. Draw a map of the area you choose. It may be your house, garage, yard, garden, or whatever area you choose. You may choose to collect the spiders as you locate them (see Collecting Spiders page 63). Unless you are very knowledgeable about spiders, identifying specific spiders is difficult. Most spiders are small and will hide if they sense danger. You may narrow down the type of spider by discovering its web. It is not essential to identify the spiders on your map; but if you do, you may need to include a key to explain your information.

Note to the teacher: Decide beforehand how large an area to map, what types of spiders and/or spider webs to look for, etc. You may decide to have your students take pictures, if possible, and make a booklet to display them along with your maps.

Spider Map

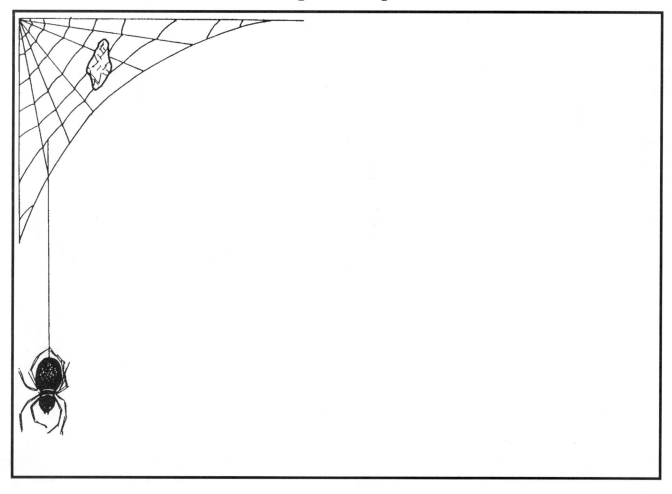

Tarantulas in the U.S.

Most tarantulas prefer a warm climate without too much rain. Research to find out which states in the United States are home to the tarantulas. Make a key to explain your information.

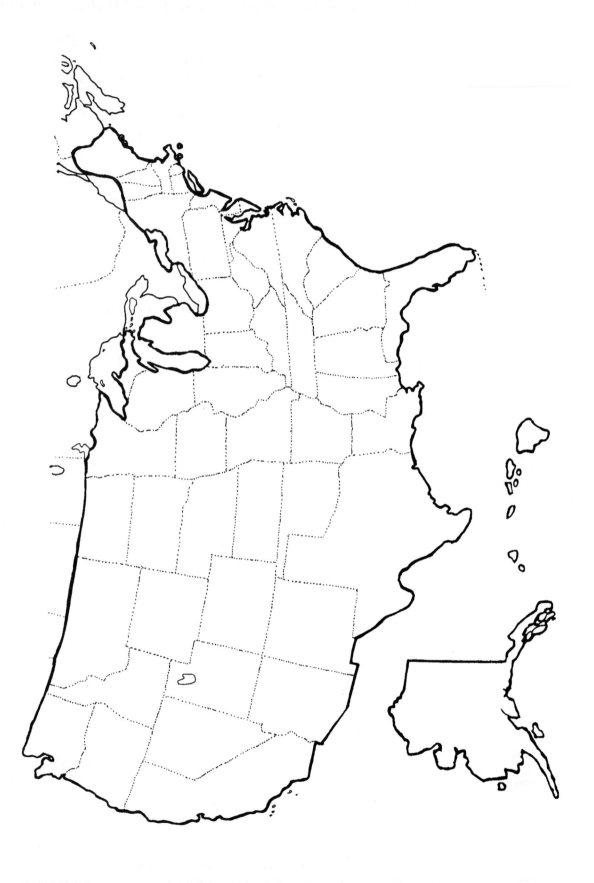

66

Spider Superstitions

How many of you have heard that handling a toad will give you warts? If the 13th day of a month falls on Friday, it is supposed to be an unlucky day. Finding a pin and picking it up is supposed to signify you will have a lucky day. These beliefs, of course, are not supported by science. They are called superstitions.

People have made up rhymes about spider superstitions. The following are some examples you may or may not have heard.

> If you wish to live and thrive,
> Let a spider run alive.

> Spot a spider in the night,
> It will bring you joy, delight.
> Spot a spider in the morning,
> Take care, for it's a warning.

Have you ever heard any superstitions about spiders or other arachnids? Have your parents? How about your grandparents? Interview someone who has, or research books, encyclopedias, etc., to find some more superstitions. Write them down to share with your classmates and put them in a booklet.

More Spider Superstitions

Living Fossils: Scorpions

Scorpions are called living fossils because they have not changed much in the past 350 million years. The earliest spiders were discovered fossilized in rocks only 300 million years old. That is slightly before our time, isn't it! A fossil from an early woman was dated at 3 million years ago. As you can see, arachnids have been around much longer than humans.

Ancient humans viewed scorpions as mystical creatures with supernatural powers. They both feared and honored them. Scorpions, like spiders, have become parts of our legends and myths. Ancient Egyptians had a scorpion-goddess. Her name was Selquet. She wore a scorpion on her head. Sometimes she was pictured as a scorpion with a woman's head.

The Greeks had a fable about Orion, the hunter. It was said that he boasted that he could kill any animal on earth. Latona and the goddess Diana did not appreciate his bragging and self-pride. For punishment, they sent a scorpion to sting Orion to death. The scorpion later was raised to heaven where it became a constellation of the zodiac called Scorpius.

Popular belief is that the sting of a scorpion means certain death. In most cases this is not true. Of the 40 or more species of scorpions in the U.S., only one, the sculptured scorpion (Centruroides sculpturatus), can cause death. But in other parts of the world, there are countries where scorpions cause a large number of deaths. So the human fear of scorpions has a real basis, especially when you discover that some countries have as many as 1,000 deaths a year, caused by scorpions.

Answer the following questions.

1. What are living fossils? _____

     _____

2. Who was Selquet? _____

     _____

3. What is Scorpius? _____

     _____

Extensions: Research to find out more about Selquet and Scorpius. Share your research with your classmates. Locate the constellations of Scorpius and Orion in the night sky.

Starchy Spider Webs

If you are not having very good luck at collecting real spider webs (see page 63), try making your own. Look in the books and magazines that you have been collecting while studying this thematic unit. Find a spider web that you would like to make, such as an orb web, triangle web, funnel web, cobweb, etc.

Here are the materials you will need:

- a styrofoam block (You need to determine how large your web will be and have an appropriate size block for it.)
- wax paper (optional)
- stick pins or thin nails
- string (various thicknesses)
- liquid starch
- a bowl or pie pan (or something similar to hold the starch into which you dip the string)
- paper towels (to clean up your mess)

Directions:

1. Draw a pattern that you intend to follow for your web. Use a pencil, marker, or crayon. Placing wax paper on your styrofoam block will ease your clean-up chores, and your styrofoam will be in better shape to be used again.

2. Place pins or nails in the styrofoam along your pattern. Allow room for wrapping or tying your string.

3. Cut pieces of string to manageable lengths.

4. Place liquid starch in a container into which you can easily dip your string.

5. With the liquid starch, cover a length of string completely.

6. Attach it to one of the pins and continue on to another. Depending on how long your string is, wrap it or tie it to another pin and continue on to the next pin in your pattern. It is something like making dot-to-dot connections for a drawing. Experiment to find out how long a string to use. You may find it easier using long pieces or, perhaps, short ones. You may decide to use different strings of various thicknesses in your pattern, just as the spiders do.

7. Allow the string to dry overnight before removing it from the pins.

8. Your stiffened webs should make good decorations in your classrooms. You may decide to hang them from branches for a touch of realism.

Don't worry if your webs are not perfect creations. Not all spiders weave perfect webs, either. (Remember the irregular cobwebs of the house spider and others.)

It's in the Stars

Have you ever looked into the sky during a sunny day and watched big puffy clouds go by? Did they look like pictures in the sky? An alligator after an ant? A bear bouncing a ball? A car crashing into a cow? They can be anything you can imagine.

The people of long ago saw the constellations as pictures in the sky. The Greeks and Romans named many of the constellations, and today we still know them by the names those ancients gave them. Have you heard of Taurus (the Bull), Canis Major (the Big Dog), Pegasus (the Winged Horse), Draco (the Dragon), Ursa Major (the Big Bear), and Ursa Minor (the Little Bear)? Those are some of them. The zodiac (circle of animals) seems to encircle the solar system. Some people not only named a constellation after a scorpion, but also made up stories to explain how it got there (see Living Fossils: Scorpions, page 68).

Creating Constellations

You can use your imagination to name your own constellations. Gaze at the sky on a starry night. What do you see?

Look at the star map on page 71, do some gazing, make some dot-to-dot connections, and name your own constellations.

Be sure to include some of the arachnids you have been studying. (For practice, complete the exercise on page 25.)

- Don't worry if your constellations are not exact replicas. Look at the constellations in the zodiac (page 71). Is Leo a lion? Is Taurus a bull?

- You can make your own star map, using gummed foil stars, markers, or crayons. Or you might use black construction paper and colored chalk. Do have fun!

- Write a story explaining how your constellation got there. You may be as imaginative as you wish—using science, science fiction, myth, fairy tale, and any original ideas that come to mind.

How My Constellation Came About

_____

_____

_____

Star Map

71

Spider Safety

Most spiders are our friends. They feed on harmful insects like flies (which can spread disease) and sowbugs (which harm plantlife).

However, the black widow and brown recluse are two dangerous spiders among those native American species which bite people. All spiders produce venom when they bite, but these two inject a poison strong enough to harm humans.

If you think you have been bitten by a black widow or brown recluse, contact your doctor or local poison control center right away.

Doctors know how to treat such bites with various antibiotics, anti-venoms, antihistamines, and cortisone.

Black Widow

- Appearance: shiny black with red or orange hourglass figure on the underside
- Size: about one-half inch (12 mm)
- Habitat: lives in dark garages, outbuildings, piles of debris, under furniture

Brown Recluse

- Appearance: brown body with a dark violin-shaped figure on its top side
- Size: about one-half inch (12 mm), similar to the black widow
- Habitat: lives in folds of clothing and also in the same places as the black widow

Danger Signs

- red, swollen, painful bite
- nausea, vomiting
- muscle cramps
- joint pains
- breathing problems

First Aid

- Keep the head lower than the bite.
- Apply ice or a cold compress.
- Apply baking-soda-and-water paste.

Household Hazards

As we know, most spiders are good friends to the gardener because they keep down the population of harmful insects. If you find a friendly spider in your house, instead of harming the little fellow, capture and release it into your garden to dine on crickets and other plant-eating creatures.

Most people, however, do not really want spiders in their homes, no matter how beneficial they might be. For this reason, many homemakers use two methods of keeping the house free of spiders (and other unwanted insect guests).

1. Clean debris from around the house, garage, basement, attic and crawl spaces, sweeping all webs away with a broom, mop, or vacuum cleaner.

2. Use insecticides, herbicides, insect repellent, no-pest strips, ant/roach killer, and rat/mouse poison.

The second method of control brings with it some dangers as unwelcome as the very spiders, insects, and pests one seeks to eliminate. Take an inventory of your house, listing the names, chemical contents, locations, poison warnings, and antidotes for any such controls. (It is wise to avoid poisonous spiders, but also wise to avoid household poisons!) List your inventory below and discuss it with your family.

Name of Poison	Chemical Contents	Location	Warnings	Antidote
1.				
2.				
3.				
4.				
5.				
6.				
7.				
8.				
9.				
10.				

Ballooning Journey

The story of *Charlotte's Web* ends with Charlotte's children leaving the barn by the dozens. They leave on the warm updraft. The spiderlings spin a cloud of fine silk. The silk forms a balloon. A breeze takes them into the air. The air is so full of the balloonists that it looks like mist. They are off to wherever the wind will take them. High, low. Near, far. East, west. North, south. Wouldn't you like to know where they ended up?

Perhaps the perfect way to end this thematic unit is to send off your own balloons. No, you don't have to fly with them.

Find a source for helium balloons. Fill out the form on the bottom of this page, laminate it or place it in a sealed plastic bag to protect it from the weather. Attach it to your balloon. Check with local authorities before releasing any and then have a balloon launch. With any luck you will get some responses when your balloons land, and you will know where the wind took you.

Hi! My name is _____

I go to this school: _____

This is the address: _____

We have been studying spiders and other arachnids in our class. We are in the _____ grade. Some spiders travel by ballooning. We wonder where they go. Will you help us learn about it by completing and returning the bottom part of this message?

Thank you!

Here is a spider fact that I have learned: _____

_____

Dear _____ ,

I found your balloon and card at or near the following street, city, and state

on the following date _____ .

Signed,

Bulletin Board Ideas

Spiders
Enlarge the diagram of the spider (page 11). Identify the various parts. Display appropriate papers from this section of our thematic unit.

Widow Spiders Around the World
Enlarge the world map (page 64). Include the same information required in the exercise. Display appropriate papers.

Tarantulas in the U.S.
Enlarge the U.S. map (page 66). On the map, place locations of tarantulas found throughout the U.S. Display appropriate papers.

Enjoy a "Wheel" Good Book
Display Wheel Books students have made (page 44).

Our Reports Are in Great Shape!
Display Shape Books from page 44.

We're Hanging Around
Display starchy spider webs (page 69).

Spiders in Our Neighborhood
Enlarge the project on page 65. Include for display any reports appropriate for this project.

Venn Diagram
Enlarge the Venn diagram (page 12) about spiders and insects. Display appropriate papers.

Constellation Creations
Display myths and constellations for It's in the Stars (page 70) and Constellation Creations (page 25).

Arachnid Journeys
Make a bar graph to show the extra material read and reported on by each student from the collection of books, magazines, and pamphlets assembled for this thematic unit. Include any other appropriate material students gathered from word bank listings (page 48), the bibliography (page 77), or the school or public library. Use the spider web or spider pattern (pages 45–46) after shrinking it to the appropriate size in a copy machine. Let either of them represent one report. You can use different colors to represent whether the report comes from an entire book or an article from a book or magazine.

Awards

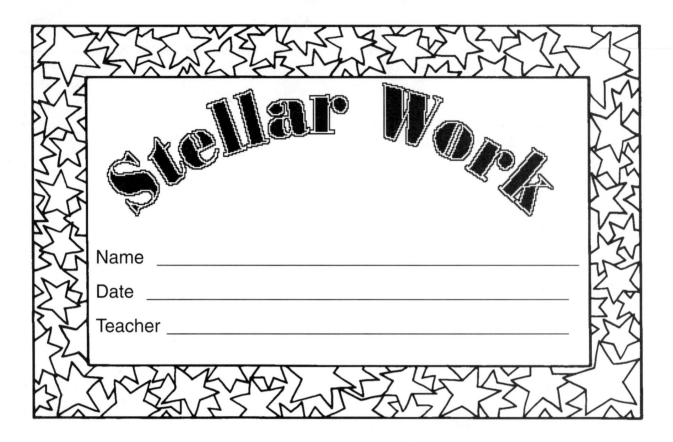

Bibliography

Arachnids

ABC's of Nature. Reader's Digest Association, 1984.

The Audubon Society Field Guide to North American Insects & Spiders. Alfred A. Knopf, Inc., 1980.

Back, Christine. *Spider's Web.* Silver Burdett Co., 1986.

Bason, Lillian. *Spiders.* National Geographic Society, 1974.

Berger, Melvin. *Stranger Than Fiction: Killer Bugs.* Avon Books, 1990.

Billings, Charlene W. *Scorpions.* Dodd, Mead & Co., 1983.

Dallinger, Jane. *Spiders.* Lerner Publication Co., 1981.

Hogner, Dorothy Childs. *Spiders.* Thomas Y. Crowell Co., 1955.

Lane, Margaret. *The Spider.* The Dial Press, 1982.

Lavine, Sigmund A. *Wonders of the Spider World.* Dodd, Mead & Co., 1966.

Levi, Herbert W. & Lorna R. *Spiders and Their Kin.* Golden Press Western Publishing Co., 1987.

Mell, Jan. *The Scorpion.* (Crestwood House) Macmillan Publishing, 1990.

Nielsen, Nancy J. *The Black Widow Spider.* Crestwood House, 1990.

Parker, Bertha Morris. *Spiders.* Row, Peterson, & Co., 1950.

Sanford, Willian R. & Carl R. Green. *The Tarantulas.* Crestwood House, 1987.

Souza, D.M. *Eight Legs.* Carolrhoda Books, Inc., 1991.

Challenging Books

Crompton, John. *The Life of the Spider.* Houghton Mifflin, 1951.

Mullett, G.M. *Spider Woman Stories.* The University of Arizona Press, 1980.

Preston-Mafham, Rod & Ken. *Spiders of the World.* Facts on File Publications, 1984.

Folk Tales

Arnott, Kathleen. *African Myths and Legends.* Henry Z. Walck, 1963.

Barlow, Genevieve. *Latin American Tales.* Rand McNally & Co., 1966.

Caduto, Michael J. & Joseph Bruchac. *Keepers of the Earth.* Fulcrum, Inc., 1988. 398.2 + PROF.

Courlander, Harold & George Herzog. *The Cow-Tail Switch.* Henry Holt & Co., 1957. 398.2 COU

Sherlock, Phillip M. *Anansi, the Spider Man.* Thomas Y. Crowell, 1954. 398.2 SHE

Tales of Nature. Steck-Vaughn, 1990.

Tales of Wonder. Steck-Vaughn, 1990.

Wood, Leigh Hope. *The Navajo Indians.* Chelsea House, 1991.

Other Fiction

White, E.B. *Charlotte's Web.* Harper & Row, 1980.

Parsons, Alexandra   Amazing Spiders   595.4 PAR

Kirk, David   ✓ Ms Spider's Tea Party   E KIR
✓ Little Miss Spider   E KIR

Answer Key

page 8

1. cephalothorax
2. spinnerets
3. abdomen
4. cocoons
5. threads
6. venom
7. molting
8. spiderling
9. insects
10. arachnids

page 10

A=495
B=633
C=130
D=204
E=192
F=101
G=9
H=47
I=244
J=56
K=112
L=568
M=45
N=90
O=51
P=117
Q=232
R=728

S=59
T=345
U=338
V=559
W=37
X=12
Y=451
Z=630

1. weavers
2. prey
3. tube
4. signal
5. humans
6. burrow
7. nature
8. eyes
9. grow
10. ballooning

page 11

1. cephalothorax & abdomen
2. neither
3. to paralyze or kill their victims
4. No. Some is sticky; some stronger than others
5. 8
6. 8 normally; some have 6, 4, 2, or none

page 15

1. arachnids
2. abdomen
3. hairs
4. jaws
5. venom
6. breathe
7. molting
8. dragline
9. ballooning
10. hunters
11. color
12. bigger

page 16

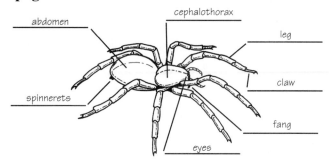

1. (1) Yes. The brown recluse and black widow.
2. (3) The female
3. (4,6) Yes. If hungry, black widow females will eat their mates and also recently hatched spiderlings.
4. (8) Telescopes, gunsights, laboratory and surveying equipment.
5. (7) Males — 4 months; females — about a year
6. (9) No.
7. (3) Theridiidae, the comb-footed spider
8. (2) 5

page 17

1. garden
2. house
3. zebra
4. crab
5. wolf
6. fishing
7. harvestmen
8. scorpions
9. whipscorpions
10. mites
11. ticks

page 18

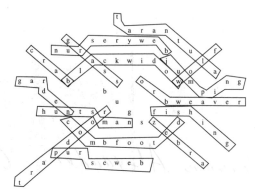

Answer Key *(cont.)*

page 27 3, 7, 1, 10, 4, 5, 9, 8, 6, 2

page 28

1. T	6. F
2. T	7. F
3. F	8. T
4. F	9. F
5. T	10. T

page 50

```
G A R D E N S P I D E R C X Y F Z
D W O O O D T I K C E R H A V I B
A S P I D S P I D E R M I T E S C
D D S C O R P I O N E S T G Q L H L
D D H A R V E S T M E N N G Q V I H
Y T A R A N T U L A S E E R E I N I
L B W H I B L A C K T A R H C T S G M
O A H I P U S P M I T E H C E M P I
N C I H N U M P M I T E O L I S G
G K P W O O D T I C K Z U U T I I
L S N O B X S I T D A D D Y E D N
E P S O O E H O U S E S P I D E R
G I O D V E S T S P I R D E R R T
S C T R P I O N A B D O M E A L S
A R A V E L V E C R A B H O U S P
W H I P S C O R P I O N L I S P Y
C H I G G B L A C K W I D O W I D
V E L V E T S C O R P I N A R T R
```

page 35

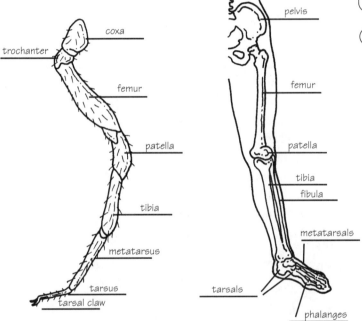

coxa
trochanter
femur
patella
tibia
metatarsus
tarsus
tarsal claw

pelvis
femur
patella
tibia
fibula
metatarsals
tarsals
phalanges

page 52

1. know	8. sense
2. eight	9. to
3. seem	10. prey
4. see	11. some
5. be	12. or
6. there	13. males
7. In	14. scent

page 53

grasshopper

page 49

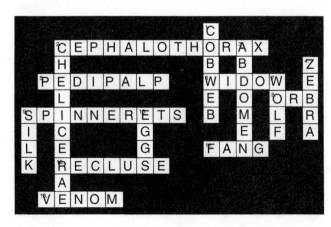

C
CEPHALOTHORAX
H   B   B   Z
PEDIPALP   WIDOW   E
L   E   O   ORB
SPINNERETS B   M   L   R
I C   G   E   F   A
L E   G   FANG
K RECLUSE
   A
VENOM

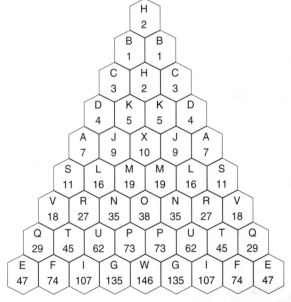

```
        H
        2
      B   B
      1   1
    C   H   C
    3   2   3
  D   K   K   D
  4   5   5   4
 A  J  X  J  A
 7  9 10  9  7
S  L  M  M  L  S
11 16 19 19 16 11
 V  R  N  O  N  R  V
18 27 35 38 35 27 18
Q  T  U  P  P  U  T  Q
29 45 62 73 73 62 45 29
E  F  I  G  W  G  I  F  E
47 74 107 135 146 135 107 74 47
```

Answer Key *(cont.)*

page 54 Cross spider or garden spider.

page 55

1. 3x8	= 24	S	A	90÷5	= 18
2. 3x6	= 18	P		6x4	= 24
3. 4x7	= 28		R	15+21	= 36
4. 4x9	= 36			143-115	= 28
5. 5x8	= 40	A	I	120÷3	= 40
6. 6x7	= 42	C		35+13	= 48
7. 6x8	= 48			21x2	= 42
8. 6x9	= 54	D	H	75-21	= 54
9. 7x7	= 49		N	21x3	= 63
10. 7x8	= 56	O		98÷2	= 49
11. 7x9	= 63			33+23	= 56
12. 8x4	= 32		P	141-109	= 32
13. 8x8	= 64	E		380-299	= 81
14. 8x9	= 72		H	50+50-100	= 0
15. 9x9	= 81	O		25x4	= 100
16. 10x0	= 0		B	136-72	= 64
17. 10x10	= 100	I		6x2	= 12
18. 100x10	= 1000	R		72x1	= 72
19. 11x2	= 22	A		66÷3	= 22
20. 12x1	= 12	S		999+1	= 1000

page 56

1. 40,000		6. 25		11. 1,000
2. 8		7. 15		12. 400
3. 0		8. 1/2		13. 700
4. 3		9. 2.000		14. 200
5. 1		10. 10		15. 20,000

page 57

1. arthopoda	7. courtship
2. arachnids	8. die
3. cephalothorax	9. egg
4. brain	10. exoskeleton
5. silk glands	11. females
6. spinnerets	12. six

page 58

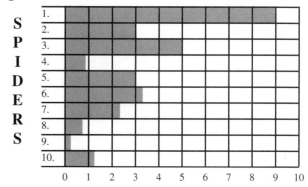

1. tarantula
2. dwarf
3. 2.5 cm
4. trap-door & purse web
5. 40mm/4 cm
6. spitting & American house
7. >
8. <
9. <
10. >

page 62

¹C	²H	I	G	G	E	R				
	A									
	R									
	V									
	E				³T		⁴I			
	⁵S	C	O	R	P	I	O	N		
	T				C		S			
	⁶M	I	T	E	K		⁷E	I	G	H	T
	E						C			
	N						T			
							⁸S	P	I	D	E	R

page 68

1. Answers will vary. Scorpions are called living fossils because their appearance has changed little in over 350 million years.

2. An Egyptian goddess.

3. A constellation of the Zodiac.